Advance Praise for *Being There*

"A must-read for young women struggling with the inner conflict between mothering and career-making. Komisar brilliantly distills the potency of present mothering from her experience as a psychoanalyst and parenting coach. She also evokes the emotional pain of babies and toddlers when their mothers are often absent or inattentive and the 'wormhole to adolescence' where all those unresolved losses will be replayed at a more punishing stage. I only wish that I and many driven career women of my early feminist generation had read this essential guide before we sacrificed Being There to proving ourselves in a man's world."

—Gail Sheehy, author of *Passages* and *Daring: My Passages*

"*Being There* is a terrific and very timely book that is much needed as our country is dealing with an epidemic of emotionally troubled children, adolescents, and mothers. Well-written and researched with excellent documentation from respected experts in this field, it should be read not only by current and prospective mothers and fathers, but also by those who care for young children in a variety of settings."

—Thomas McInerny MD, FAAP, past president of the American Academy of Pediatrics

"It's hard to believe, but the United States is actually behind, well behind, the rest of the world in maternity leave policy. We all, not just the mothers, fathers, and children, pay dearly for this. In this book, Erica Komisar provides hard-headed and practical advice for families and policy makers. It is a rare and valuable contribution to the field."

—Leslie H. Gelb, president emeritus of the Council on Foreign Relations

"It should not take a psychoanalyst to explain the importance of maternal love and support in the formation of a child, but Erica Komisar in her book *Being There* does just that, cutting through the head-spinning Mommy Wars that have haunted this generation of parents. Her challenging assessment that absent and distracted mothers leave their children forever less happy will upset apple carts and give many overtaxed young parents pause, but she accompanies her tough medicine with realistic tools and strategies to help caregivers meet their challenging task. Komisar's book is difficult but necessary reading for any parent-to-be."

—Eric L. Motley, Ph.D., executive vice president of the Aspen Institute

"*Being There* is a mindful and honest approach to both the joys and challenges of motherhood. This must-read guidebook for stay-at-home and working mothers shows us how to be present not only for our babies but for our lives."

—Mary T. Cantwell, co-director of the Garden House School of New York

"Here's the problem. That beautiful baby doesn't arrive with a how-to manual in his chubby arms, and I'd come to believe that there is no right way to bring up a child. But along comes Erica Komisar, a warm and experienced psychoanalyst, with the key to the puzzle of how to achieve two things at once: a kid set to become a happy, emotionally secure person, and a mother who is effective and fulfilled. It happens, simply, by 'being there' most of the time throughout the first three years of a baby's life. If you think this isn't for you, just read this book and think again. Nobody said it would be easy."

—Marilyn Berger Hewitt, broadcast journalist, contributing writer to the *Washington Post* and *New York Times*, and author of *This Is a Soul*

"*Being There* is a courageous, bold, and invaluable book that challenges us to consider our roles as mothers. Erica Komisar has written a beautiful book that pushes the reader to consider how to be the best possible mother she can be while supporting her through the process."

—Carly Snyder, M.D., host of the weekly radio show *MD for Moms*

"The beauty and practical value of Ms. Komisar's book is that she gives specific suggestions on how women can be more emotionally present for their child regardless of their career, financial constraints and the amount of time they can spend with their children. A must-read for parents, mental health professionals, and childcare policy makers."

—Dr. Ellen Jacobs, child and adolescent psychotherapist, adjunct professor at the Columbia University School of Social Work

"Timely and highly informative. Using the direct voices of the most important scientists in the field, Erica Komisar describes in clear and compelling fashion the foundational events of the early years, an unparalleled time of growth of the baby's right brain that is indelibly shaped by the maternal relationship. In addition to providing practical and very personal information to the reader on how to be 'the best, most present mother she can be,' this gifted psychotherapist also offers controversial political implications of advances in the developmental sciences for the mental and physical health of future generations. This rich amalgam of science, clinical wisdom, and common sense represents a Dr. Spock for the twenty-first century, and is quite simply the best book I've ever seen on this absolutely essential topic."

—Allan N. Schore, Ph.D., Department of Psychiatry and Biobehavioral Sciences, University of California, Los Angeles, David Geffen School of Medicine

BEING THERE

Why Prioritizing Motherhood in the First Three Years Matters

ERICA KOMISAR, LCSW

with Sydny Miner

A TarcherPerigee Book

tarcherperigee

An imprint of Penguin Random House LLC
375 Hudson Street
New York, New York 10014

Most TarcherPerigee books are available at special quantity discounts
for bulk purchase for sales promotions, premiums, fund-raising, and educational needs.
Special books or book excerpts also can be created to fit specific needs.
For details, write: SpecialMarkets@penguinrandomhouse.com.

ISBN 9780143109297

Printed in the United States of America
1 3 5 7 9 10 8 6 4 2

Book design by Elke Sigal

To my incredible husband, Jordan, my best friend and my inspiration, whose love and support made this book possible, and to my beautiful children, Bryce, Jonas, and Sofia, who have taught me more than I have taught them. I am grateful to be their mother each and every day. And to my mother, Edith, who valued mothering over everything else; your warmth, affection, and nurturing have been my example.

Children are not a distraction from more important work.
They are the most important work.

—C. S. LEWIS

Your children need your presence more than your presents.

—JESSE JACKSON

There is no way to be a perfect mother and a million ways to
be a good one.

—JILL CHURCHILL

CONTENTS

PART 3 • CHANGING THE CONVERSATION

INTRODUCTION

Ten years ago I began writing a book about what happens to children when their mothers devalue, deprioritize, and neglect mothering. Then I realized that I would have to postpone the project because it would mean my book would be my primary focus instead of my being fully present for my children.

Now my children are preteens and teenagers and are out of the house for much of the day during the week, attending school, participating in other activities, and seeing friends. I am still present for my children when they are home, but as my teenage son walks in the door and gives me a hug, I realize that it's my presence, not my focused attention that he needs, as he did when he was younger. My children have lives apart from our family, and although they still need me, I don't have to attend to their physical and emotional needs with the same intensity. I have more time during the day and more mental space. And that, I realized, is the point of this book.

The truth is, we can do everything in life, but not at the same time. We cannot raise healthy children if we are not there for them emotionally and physically. We cannot be present for them while being intensely involved with work or other interests that make us less mindful of and attentive to the emotional needs of our children.

I am deeply saddened by the mommy wars still raging across this country between working and nonworking mothers, because rather than supporting *all* mothers, we have created a divisive environment. Like every mother, whether she works outside the home or not, I am faced with the challenge of regulating and balancing my own needs with those of my children, and as a working mother, I made decisions about when to return to work and how many hours to work when my children were very young. And while this is a book about the well-being of our children, it is also about the happiness and well-being of their mothers. We can have all the career success we have ever dreamed of, but every mother knows that when our children suffer, we suffer too. If we have all the career success in the world but our children resent us or, worse, are disabled by our insensitivity or lack of empathy toward their needs when they are young and become depressed, anxious, or cannot form and sustain deep emotional connections with others, are we truly satisfied as mothers? So many parents constantly feel guilty because they are stretched too thin, torn between conflicting obligations, and not able to give the time and energy they want to all of them. I think there is a solution, but it requires mothers and fathers to examine their core values and make their family a priority and that we, as a society, become more child-centric. We need to understand and respect the unique and essential place a mother has in her child's life, especially in the first three years.

I am a psychoanalyst in private practice in New York City, and for the past twenty-four years, I have been focused on mother–child relationships, first as a social worker, then a parent guidance expert and psychoanalyst, treating children and adults for problems related to early relationship loss and trauma; behavioral and developmental issues in young children; and depression, anxiety, and addictions of all kinds in older children and young adults. From my firsthand professional observations, I have come to understand the connections between these symptoms and disorders and the emotional and physical absence of young children's mothers in their day-to-day lives. An increasing number of parents come to see me because their child is suffering from a variety of social, behavioral, or developmental disorders.

It's clear to me that these symptoms are often related to the premature separation of children from their mothers. These are women who, despite their best intentions, and whether they stay at home or work outside the home, may not know how to be present for their child or how to recognize the signs that their child is in distress.

As a therapist, I am in the business of making people feel uncomfortable so they can change and ultimately live happier and more satisfying lives. You may not like what I am going to say in this book. If you're already a mother or you're contemplating having children, it may make you feel guilty or uncomfortable. If you are contemplating having a child, I hope it will inspire greater self-awareness about the choices you face.

There is enough research, statistical evidence, and case material from my own work and that of my colleagues to make a strong argument that as a society we are failing our children: There has been a dramatic increase in emotional, social, and behavioral difficulties like ADHD, anxiety, depression, and increased aggression in children from toddlerhood through adolescence.

The statistics are frightening. According to the Centers for Disease Control and Prevention (CDC), 11 percent of children between the ages of four and seventeen years in the United States have been diagnosed with ADHD. This is a dramatic 16 percent increase since 2007. In addition, two-thirds of those children were treated with stimulant medications, like Ritalin and Adderall, both of which have significant side effects.[1]

In a 2011 data brief describing key findings from the 2005–2008 National Health and Nutrition Examination Surveys, the CDC reported there has been a 400 percent increase of prescriptions for antidepressant medications to children over the age of twelve years since 1988. In fact, 11 percent of Americans over the age of twelve now take antidepressants. From 2011 to 2012 the number of teenagers prescribed generic drugs for psychiatric disorders jumped to 19.4 percent. In younger children, the number diagnosed with psychiatric disorders rose to a staggering 19 percent.[2]

Eating disorders are also on the rise. A study from the Agency for Healthcare Research and Quality stated that more than 25 million people in the United States suffer from an eating disorder,[3] and hospitalizations of children twelve years and under for eating disorders has increased 119 percent in the last decade.[4]

Another disturbing trend is the increase in violence, aggression, and bullying in children of all ages, as demonstrated in a 2011 survey reported by the CDC:

- More than 700,000 young people aged ten to twenty-four years were treated in emergency departments for nonfatal injuries sustained from assaults.

- About 33 percent of high school students reported being in a physical fight in the twelve months before the survey.

- Approximately 20 percent of high school students reported being bullied on school property, and 16 percent reported being bullied electronically.[5]

Why is this happening to our children? One key factor, I believe, is that because so many of us are ambitiously pursuing our own individual needs, we forget how we evolved as social creatures. Too often, mothers are putting their work and their own needs ahead of their children's. I know this issue is a very controversial one—so controversial, in fact, that few dare to address it. Colleagues and researchers write about children and their primary caregivers and won't use the word *mother*. Clinicians are reluctant to make direct correlations publicly between an emotionally disengaged or physically absent mother and a child's personality, social functioning, and even mental illness, but it is what we discuss as clinicians among ourselves. A growing body of evidence from neuroscience and hormonal, attachment, and epigenetic research supports the link that we have seen in our clinical practices. It is also an issue about which I have always felt strongly. For years, I've been motivated to create change—social change, not just psychological change in a few; it's why I was a social worker before I went into private practice as a psychoanalyst.

We see extensive discussion in the media about the needs of working parents, but the subject of children's needs is noticeably missing from the conversation. For example, in a recent article in the *New York Times*, "Wall Street Mothers, Stay-Home Fathers,"[6] we learn about parents reshuffling their roles as provider and caregiver, but we don't hear how these power couples' children feel when their mothers are not present. Nor do we hear much about how these parents deal with their conflicted feelings over leaving their very young children in the care of others. It seems that few of us want to talk about what is best for our children—or the fact that what is best for our children is also best for their mothers and fathers in the long run. In this book I will talk about what is good for our children and what is good for women's success and satisfaction in one conversation.

Emotional and physical neglect, and the suffering that results from it, may be the most common reason people enter psychotherapy. Freud said, "Repeating is remembering," which is a nice way of saying that although we may forget the painful experiences in our own childhood, we often re-create the patterns of our upbringing with our own children. In his poem "This Be the Verse," Philip Larkin said it well:

They fuck you up, your mum and dad.
They may not mean to, but they do.
They fill you with the faults they had
And add some extra, just for you.

But they were fucked up in their turn
By fools in old-style hats and coats,
Who half the time were soppy-stern
And half at one another's throats.

Man hands on misery to man.
It deepens like a coastal shelf.
Get out as early as you can,
And don't have any kids yourself.

If we took Larkin's words to heart, very few of us would have children at all. But what I think he is really trying to tell us is that mothers who were hurt by the way their mother nurtured them will often create the same pattern with their own children and pass their parenting styles, and the pain they felt, to the next generation. But we *can* change this pattern, and I will show you how to make the changes that will make all the difference to your children, and bring greater joy to you too.

This book explores what I see as a major social issue of our time: the effects of maternal absence on our children. I want to encourage mothers to be more present and self-aware and to seek the support and help they need. I write this book for all of the voiceless children who are suffering from their mother's absence, both emotionally and physically, and for all the mothers who feel pain and conflict when leaving their children. There is another way.

PART 1

A MOTHER'S PRESENCE

CHAPTER 1

More Is More

Raising children is not an adventure in minimalism. We're not just talking about stuff—toys, baby gear, stuffed animals; during the first three years of your child's life the more time, attention, and focus you can give her, the better. Dr. Thomas K. McInerny, past president of the American Academy of Pediatrics, said, "Frequent positive interaction between a mother and her baby in the first three years of life is critically important for the child's social and cognitive development." Your nurturing presence in your child's early years affects the development of her brain.[1] A new study released by the Stanford University School of Medicine showed that a child's brain responds more strongly to her mother's voice than the voices of strangers; the brain regions engaged are involved not just with auditory processing but also with emotion and social function, among others.[2] Spending more time with your child during this critical period of development means she will have a greater chance of being emotionally secure and resilient to stress as well as being better able to regulate her emotions throughout life, read others' social cues, achieve a higher emotional intelligence, and connect with others intimately.

But a mother's physical presence in itself is not enough. What *is* vital for both the short-term and long-term well-being of your child is your emotional presence. And I want to stress that without physical presence—if you are not with your child—you cannot be emotionally present. And just as time spent with your child has long-term benefits, the lack of that essential connection can have lifelong repercussions.

Am I saying that expectant and new mothers should quit their jobs and discard their career goals? That mothers who work outside the home or spend time at the gym, volunteering, or with friends are condemning their children to a life of emotional and social distress? That mothers should devote 100 percent of their waking hours to their children? I'm not. It is more complicated than that.

However, it is indisputable that the first three years present a crucial, formative window. There's substantial research that confirms the more time a woman can devote to the joy and job of mothering during that period, the better the chance her child will be emotionally secure and healthy throughout his life. If it's possible to put a career on hold, if it's possible to work part-time, or if it's possible to work from home some or all of the time, I believe that is an exchange worth making. Of course many women, including single mothers and women whose partners cannot support their families alone, may have few choices about whether to work or to stay home. No matter what choices you make, in this book you'll find concrete ways to maximize the time you do have with your child and to be as present as possible; I also provide advice for selecting and guiding a caregiver.

I understand these decisions are not simple. There are a number of issues women consider when they're deciding how to prioritize family and work: the burden of financial concerns, the importance of independence from their partner, the negative effects on their career, the fear of being bored with their baby, and the worry of being a "bad" mother.

Our society values financial security and material success over the more important values of emotional security and connection to those closest to us. Are we making the right choice when we choose a more comfortable material life over the mental health and well-being of our children and ourselves? Your baby does not care if she has a bigger room or a Florida vacation; what she wants is you and the safety and security of being in your presence. What I hope this book will do is inspire you to question whether you *need* or *want* more financial resources and whether this critical time in your baby's life is when you should be focusing on professional and material success.

Yes, there are often career costs associated with taking time off or scaling back your work hours while your child (or children) are young. This is reality. When we make the commitment to have children, we also need to make the commitment to care for them, and that involves making sacrifices. Some of these sacrifices may include accepting that we may have less money and more expenses, a changing relationship with our spouse or partner, less time with friends, and less time for ourselves. If we can let go of the fear of losing out on our careers and realize that the time we spend with our children is, as Jacalyn S. Burke said, cash in their emotional trust fund[3] and an investment in their future, we can look differently at how we spend our valuable resources.

Having a baby can be a transformative experience; nothing in a woman's life will ever be the same again. When we have a child, we have to learn to let go of preconceptions and unrealistic expectations about what we can and cannot do. In my practice, I hear many women talk about their fears of "losing themselves" when they become mothers. They're afraid of losing their identity and independence and of needing to depend, emotionally and financially, on their partner or spouse. They mourn the loss of their former lives, which is a natural and appropriate response to the seismic shift that has taken place. The problem arises when a mother is in denial about the changes she must adapt to and what her child needs to thrive. This is reflected in a need to have her children be independent and separate before they are developmentally ready.

Many women say they are bored taking care of their children and use this as their argument against being more present: How can they be a good mother if they don't enjoy being with their children? Every relationship and every job has boring moments. However, when a woman's overwhelming feeling when she is with her child is disinterest or boredom, it is a sign of difficulty in the mother–child relationship. If your own mother took no joy in mothering and was distracted, disinterested, and/or depressed, then you too may struggle with mothering. But the good news is that you can heal yourself and your relationship with your baby if you make the effort to become more self-aware, and to spend more time with and pay attention to your baby.

There is little support or encouragement for women who may be considering taking time off or scaling back their work when they have children. In fact, quite the opposite. Instead of universal paid leave for new parents, we have a patchwork system that varies from state to state, and sometimes company to company. Most corporate cultures pressure new parents to return to work as soon as possible and resist offering flextime and other creative options for women and men who want to make their children a priority, even for a limited amount of time. Companies and the government can do more by creating extended maternity leave policies, supported by legislation, and offering flexible and part-time work. The Mommy Track has become a dirty word, when it could—and should—be a way for employers to retain valuable workers and offer them a way back to additional responsibility when they are ready to focus more of their time and energy on work.

I look at this book as the start of a conversation that will raise awareness of what's at stake when we ignore the consequences of our choices. We all need more—more connection, more reflection, more self-awareness—so we can give our children all they need—more time with the people they love and need, more nurturing, more attention. I hope that women and men, as well as policymakers and employers, will participate in this conversation, recognizing the essential role of mothers in the lives of their children and making it easier for women to be there when it matters most.

CHAPTER 2

Debunking the Myths of Modern Motherhood

Making Better Choices

Is there any role for a woman that generates more opinions, discussion, and controversy than motherhood? We're bombarded with conflicting messages, advice, expectations, and dictates from experts, family, friends, and the media. Some of what we're told is true, but much of what we believe—or are told to believe—is not. When we buy into these pervasive myths, we may make decisions about our life priorities that have a negative effect on our families and ourselves.

The one universal truth about motherhood is that it is the hardest yet most rewarding job anyone can take on. Motherhood is not a requirement or an obligation but a privilege that comes with great responsibility and great joy. The biological ability to have a child and the ability to be a good mother are not the same thing. Many women have children without understanding the intensity of the commitment needed to care for those children in a way that fosters healthy emotional development, security, and resilience. Our children's well-being (and our own happiness as mothers) depends on our understanding of what children really need and how we can best provide for them.

Let's look at some of the most pervasive beliefs about mothering and motherhood and what the truth really is.

Myth 1: You Can Be a Perfect Mother

There is no perfect mother. There is no perfect child. Sometimes the match of a mother's and a child's personalities is a good one, and sometimes it is not. Think of the mother–baby relationship as a dance; if your and your partner's styles complement each other, you'll work more smoothly as a team. For instance, a calm and patient mother and a tranquil baby, an anxious mother who has a calm infant, or a calm and patient mother with a more fractious baby makes the process of mothering an easier one. However, often mothers' and babies' personalities are not a good fit. If a very anxious mother has a more sensitive and fractious baby or a mother who needs a great deal of contact with her baby has an infant who is more withdrawn, the woman may feel rejected, incompetent, and depressed. We have an image of what our child will be like when she is born and what we will be like as mothers, but it is not possible to predict what kind of personality your baby will have or if you and your baby will immediately find a comfortable rhythm to your relationship; what matters is how you understand, accept, and meet your child's needs, even when the match is imperfect.

It's often the case that women have very high or unrealistic expectations of what their experience of pregnancy and childbirth will be like. Many women expect that they will have no physical discomfort, uneasiness, or negative feelings about carrying and nurturing a child and that the entire time will be joyful and pleasurable. In fact, mothering has many joyful and pleasurable parts but, like all adventures in life, it also has uncomfortable bits. We may love being pregnant and feeling our baby kick but hate the feeling of being swollen or may have trouble walking. We may feel overwhelming love for our baby when we see him for the first time but hate the process of giving birth, particularly if there were complications or if we needed a C-section when we had planned for a natural birth. We may love the *idea* of breastfeeding, but the reality is that it can be at first frustrating, physically painful, and overwhelming until we (and the baby) get the hang of it.

Mothering is not a perfectible art; that is an artificial and unachievable goal, yet it is important for the well-being of our children that we *strive to be better* by doing everything we can to ensure, given our circumstances, that we give our children the best chance for emotional and physical health. We can be what pediatrician Donald Winnicott called a "good enough mother,"[1] one who focuses on her child's needs but is also a fallible human being. In an article in *Psychology Today*, Dr. Jennifer Kunst described such a woman as "a mother under pressure and strain . . . she is both selfless and self-interested. She is capable of great dedication yet she is also prone to resentment. . . . She is not boundless. She is real." Kunst went on to say, "Real mothers are the best kind of mothers (and the only kind!). It takes an imperfect mother to raise a child well."[2]

Striving to be better is at the core of being human, but striving for perfection is another thing entirely. When we strive for perfection, we are trying to meet our own parents' unmet expectations of us. *Perfect* is a word I associate with low self-esteem because it is so often used by individuals who are struggling to feel good about themselves, and in so doing, they place unrealistic standards on everything they do and are.

When my clients or friends ask me how to raise healthy children, I tell them to learn as much as they can about themselves and their feelings about their mothers before they have children and to be as empathetic and responsive to their child's needs as possible without constantly hovering. I tell them to create a community of women who can support and nurture them so they can nurture their babies. Some amount of worry is normal and necessary; too much can create feelings of anxiety in your baby.

Does this mean you won't make mistakes, do the wrong thing, or say the wrong thing? Of course not! The mother who accepts herself as imperfect uses these mistakes as a way of learning to be better; she is self-aware and looks at her past to understand her present. As I say to my own children, mistakes are a problem only if we don't learn from them. If we hurt a loved one or friend, the burden is on us to think about our actions and interactions and to make amends. It is the same with our children.

Striving to be better means being courageous, daring to do things differently from those around you because it is the right thing to do for you and your family, and knowing the goal is not to be a perfect mother or raise perfect children: It is to be the mother that your children need so they can be emotionally healthy and secure.

Myth 2: I Can Be a Good Mother Only if
I Neglect My Own Needs

Does being a mother involve sacrifice? Yes, without question. Work, family, friends, and taking care of our homes and social lives all demand our time and attention; busyness has become a badge of pride. It would be lovely if we could all have a time-turner, like Hermione Granger in *Harry Potter and the Prisoner of Azkaban*. This magical timepiece allowed her to do much more in a day than real time would allow; she could literally be in two places at once. But alas, the time-turner is a fantasy, and finding the time to do everything that our overstuffed lives require (or we think they require) seems to be an impossible task for the most organized of us.

Women are told that we can do it all—at the same time—and that's the standard to which we hold ourselves. To which I say: Baloney. Superwoman is a comic strip character, and as far as I know she didn't have children while she was saving the world. Your time and energy are not unlimited resources. Taking care of yourself requires that you reconsider and reset your priorities. You can't be a good mother if you are exhausted and depleted emotionally, mentally, and physically. For example, if you don't take some time for yourself during the course of a day and if your child struggles to fall asleep, you may be anxious and resentful. As the flight attendant tells us: Put on your own oxygen mask before you help your child put on hers.

> Your time and energy are not unlimited resources.

We say in my field that everything is about intensity and degree; if you prioritize your and your baby's well-being, then it is very difficult to work at a job that demands all of your physical, mental, and emotional energy and most of your time. If work or other commitments consume all your physical and emotional resources, what is left for you or your child?

As the mother of a baby or toddler, you may need to reconsider the amount of time and energy you commit to your job or other activities. You may need to have your partner take on additional responsibilities at home. Your house may not be ready for a white glove inspection, and on occasion dinner may be scrambled eggs or frozen pizza. So what? Babies need their mothers, and mothers need to take care of themselves so they can care for their babies; everything else is up for negotiation.

Myth 3: Stay-at-Home Mothers Are Better Than Working Mothers for a Child's Mental and Emotional Health

All mothers are working mothers; saying otherwise is one of the ways we devalue what mothers do. And let me say: I hate the term *stay-at-home mother*. A woman who chooses to spend most of her time nurturing her child is not under house arrest. She cannot, and should not, be with her child 24/7. She should find time to nourish and nurture herself, whether it's getting her nails done, taking a yoga class, or simply walking in the park. She should spend time with her friends and her partner apart from her child. If she needs or wants to return to work, she can still make her child her priority. (I'll talk more about that in Chapter 5.) When each of my children was born I took six months off from my practice, then returned to work one and a half hours a day, five days a week, often by phone. When my youngest was three years old I was working three hours a day.

All mothers are working mothers.

No mother I have ever helped did better when accused of being a bad mother; it is empathy and compassion that help all mothers be better. In a perfect world, working mothers would respect and admire stay-at-home mothers for their choice, and stay-at-home mothers would recognize that women who work (whether or not they must do so to support their family) are not abandoning their children.

A present mother is not just physically present: Presence requires being physically *and* emotionally available to your child. A mother who works long hours and sees very little of her child for days at a time will have a harder time establishing an emotional connection with that child when they are together. In their wartime nursery study,[3] Anna Freud and Dorothy Burlingham found that children who had long separations from their mothers were negatively impacted and developed symptoms, including depression and anxiety. A study by Jay Belsky and David Eggebeen published in the *Journal of Marriage and the Family* noted that children of full-time working mothers were more likely to show signs of behavior problems and insecurity than the children of mothers who were not employed during their first three years.[4]

However, a stay-at-home mother who is bored by caring for her child; inattentive to her child's needs; overwhelmed with caring for her child; distracted by her phone, tablet, or computer; or caught up in social or other family obligations—or the mother who is depressed and turns away from her child emotionally—is as absent to that child as a mother who spends long hours away from home. A 1998 study from the National Institute of Mental Health (NIMH) found that children of depressed mothers showed signs of anxiety and aggressive behavior at a much higher rate than children of well mothers.[5]

Both working and nonworking mothers should strive to be as present *as much as possible* in the first three years of their child's life and be willing and able to quickly repair the mother–child bond when they return from a separation. (I'll describe some techniques for this in Chapter 5.)

Myth 4: Attachment Occurs in the First Three Months

In my practice, mothers often tell me that if they spend a few weeks bonding with their baby, then they can return to work or leave their child for extended periods of time. I want to set the record straight: Attachment doesn't end after the first three months of life. Attachment is an ongoing process throughout the first year of a child's life. Studies of secure attachment showed that if an infant is insecurely attached at four months he has a greater chance of being insecurely attached at one year.[6] However, this does not mean that after four months you can leave and expect your baby to remain securely attached. Bonding may occur in the first few hours or weeks after a baby is born, but secure attachment requires continuous "split-second" maintenance in the first year, according to infant–mother researcher Dr. Daniel Stern.[7]

Bonding is similar, but not identical, to imprinting in the warm-blooded animal world. Both processes share the same goal—the recognition by the baby of the mother (or mother substitute) as a source of comfort, protection, and food. In animals, imprinting happens immediately after birth. (Of course, most animal babies are far more developed at birth than are human infants.) Konrad Lorenz, the famous zoologist and ethologist, is well-known for his experiment with baby geese. As soon as the goslings hatched they imprinted on him as their mother and followed him everywhere.[8] If only it were that simple with human beings.

Bonding is not always immediate in humans. For a woman who looks forward to being a mother, it begins when she knows she is pregnant. For a child, it begins in utero, as the baby becomes aware of his mother's voice. Once the baby is born, the process requires *time* as well as skin-to-skin contact, auditory stimulation, and eye contact between mother and baby as soon as possible after birth, but the process can take several weeks. It's worth repeating: The process of bonding may happen quickly or may take weeks, but it can't happen if you're not there. Mothers who are suffering from postpartum depression or may have suffered trauma themselves as babies or children may struggle longer than three months with this process. In some cases, a mother may never fully bond with her baby.

Attachment occurs *after* bonding takes place; the two processes are inseparable. Attachment begins in the first few months of life, but it is the *continuous* presence of the mother in the first eighteen months that is the first step in building a deep and lasting sense of emotional security in a child. This security forms the basis of a child's sense of self for the rest of her life. Bonding is putting the pieces together and attachment is gluing them in place.

Many women want to believe that they can attach to their babies immediately (and vice versa) because they have only six weeks (and sometimes less) of maternity leave. Sometimes they are afraid of being out of the office too long, either because they will lose their job or because they will be perceived as less ambitious or committed. When they don't feel like they've attached to their child, they feel like they have failed.

Attachment takes many months. Think of a sailboat tied to a dock in rough waters. The waters keep pulling the boat away from the dock, and you need to keep resecuring the boat until the worst of the storm passes. Think of the baby's first eighteen months as those rough waters and you as the dock. New mothers who have more time to attach to their babies may feel less pressure. Some mothers understand their baby right away, but others are late bloomers and take longer to learn to read their baby's cues.

This pressure to attach right away is a contributor to postpartum depression, as is the pressure to return to work quickly. When you feel you will have to leave your baby so soon, it is much harder to attach because of the anxiety caused by the pressure for it to happen by a deadline. Also, mothers often unconsciously fear getting too attached when they know they have to return to work. Imagine meeting and dating someone in America who is leaving to live in Australia in two months. How attached would you let yourself get? This is one of the great arguments among many for maternity leave policies that take into consideration the realities of the emotional development of the baby and mental health of the mother. (I discuss this in more detail in Chapter 10.)

Myth 5: In the Beginning, Any Caregiver Will Do

Mothers are unique in their connection to their babies from an instinctual, biological, and emotional perspective. From the moment
they enter the world, babies know the difference between their mothers
and everyone else. To a baby, only her mother sounds the way she does,
smells the way she does, and looks at her with the *right* eyes. Babies are
much more attuned to their environment than many mothers might
like to believe, and, as a result, a mother's presence from the very beginning is critical. In fact, babies as young as six months mourn when
their mothers are not present or leave them for long periods of time.
Psychoanalyst Melanie Klein believed that mourning is part of every
baby's experience.[9] Attachment expert John Bowlby held that separation anxiety is a normal part of development.[10] Klein also said a
mother can soften the mourning experience via her emotional
presence and availability.

James and Joyce Robertson, London-based psychoanalysts, wrote:

> If a child is taken from his mother's care at this age, when he
> is so possessively and passionately attached to her, it is indeed
> as if his world has been shattered. . . . To the child of two with
> his lack of understanding and complete inability to tolerate
> frustration it is really as if his mother had died . . . so over-
> whelming is his sense of loss.[11]

This does not mean that a child cannot have other loved ones and
caregivers who nurture and care for her when her mother is not there,
but mothers, fathers, and caregivers are *not* interchangeable.

Many researchers now use the term *primary parent* to describe a
child's primary caregiver, giving equal importance to a male or female
parent. However, this denies the unique importance of mothers to in-

fants and toddlers. When mothers are absent or nonexistent, children mourn that loss. If we are going to embrace a system in which mothers are exchanged for other caregivers, then we need to acknowledge the loss that children feel; denying this causes them additional pain. In a family (whether mixed or single sex) without a mother and in which a father is the primary parent, he must take on the role as sensitive nurturer. (I'll talk about this more in Chapter 6.)

Myth 6: Newborns Are Boring, and Besides, It's Better to Be with My Baby When She Can Interact with Me

When mothers refer to their babies as boring, I usually see it as a symptom of anxiety and depression. Many mothers prefer to be around older, more independent and interactive children because they are uncomfortable with the seemingly endless needs and dependence of infants and toddlers. This may stem from their own unresolved losses and pain from their own childhood. Regardless of the cause, it's a preference that should be examined and overcome, for the sake of both newborn and mother.

And let's be honest: Society tells women to have children, but doesn't tell them that it is the hardest (and most important) job they will ever do. Caring for a baby is exhausting, frustrating, sleepless work that requires commitment, sacrifice, and hard work beyond anything they have ever tackled. There are no long weekends or days off. In the beginning, infants require their mothers give to them constantly and unconditionally, without getting much in return. It requires the ability to tolerate great amounts of stress and pushes the limits of even the most patient mother's psyche. (I'll discuss this in more detail in Chapter 4.)

Medical and scientific advancements like antibiotics can claim responsibility for ensuring that more babies survive to become adults than in the past. In 1900, the biggest killers of children were pneumonia and influenza. Today, chronic stress-related illnesses have replaced infectious diseases as a danger to our children; early life stressors that impact an infant's physical well-being also create social, emotional, and cognitive impairments that affect her life going forward.[12]

For the first few weeks it may *seem* like a baby does nothing but eat, poop, and sleep. But the truth is very different; an infant is creating 40,000 synapses (connections between neurons in the brain) *per second*.[13] One of the biggest myths is that newborns don't smile until they're about six weeks old and that anything you see that looks like a smile is actually gas. In fact, as early as forty-two hours after birth, a baby has the ability to imitate others: If you smile at your baby, your baby will smile back at you. This mirroring is the basis for communication and empathy. Your baby's brain doubles in size during the first year of life. This extraordinary brain growth is, according to Dr. Allan Schore, professor of interpersonal neurobiology at the Geffen School of Medicine at UCLA, "experience dependent"—that is "reliant on social interaction" with the mother.[14]

The relationship between mother (or a primary caregiver) and an infant is built on nuanced and subtle interactions; it requires patience and careful attention to a baby's cues. This kind of patience and calm waiting are *not* qualities our modern society values or teaches; on the contrary, it requires speed, obvious results, and progress, not nuance and sensitivity.

Myth 7: If I'm Bored Taking Care of My Baby, It's Better to Have Someone Who Enjoys It Care for Him

This is both true and a myth.

When a mother leaves her infant to return to work, she might do so because of external pressure—a societal or cultural expectation, perceived financial need, or financial necessity—or an internal conflict that makes her anxious and fearful that she will not be able to nurture her child.

It is my belief that it is best for a child to have his mother as his primary caregiver and for her to be emotionally and physically present for as much of his first three years as possible. This does not mean she must be with him every minute of every day or actively engaged and interacting with him every minute he is awake, and it does not mean a mother should not work outside the home. But science has shown us that the more time a mother can spend with her baby during that time, the happier and more emotionally and physically healthy that baby will be.

No one is perfect; it's normal to feel bored, frustrated, or even a little ambivalent about being a mother *sometimes*. But when boredom, ambivalence, and frustration are the primary feelings that a mother has toward her child and her role as a caregiver, leaving her child is a way to avoid those uncomfortable feelings. Our society validates her decision by telling her that her feelings are both reasonable and acceptable. In fact, pervasive boredom and ambivalence are often signs of anxiety and postpartum depression, which should be addressed rather than accepted and brushed aside.

Boredom can be a signal feeling, a red flag that something is wrong and should not be ignored but given serious attention. When a pediatrician or nurse practitioner hears a new mother say, "I am bored," it should be a sign that the mother needs help and may not have bonded and attached to her baby. I will discuss this in a later chapter, but suffice to say that if a mother is feeling bored with her baby, she needs help with her feelings rather than being encouraged to turn away from them and rush back to work or other activities.

Many people in my field would say a baby who is cared for by a happy caregiver is better off than a baby who is home with a mother who would rather be someplace else, for whatever reason. I don't disagree in principle, but I also don't believe that we should give up on this critical relationship so quickly. This is the time that the hard work with mothers should begin. Rather than encourage mothers to leave their babies in the care of others when they are depressed, we should help those mothers deal with their depression and do what we can to facilitate the attachment process: While babies and children need a primary caregiver who enjoys the experience of caring for them, it is best if that caregiver who enjoys them is their mother.

However, if a mother is severely depressed or has been so traumatized by her own experiences and losses that she cannot or will not care for her child or is at risk of harming herself and/or her child, then an alternative caregiver is not only appropriate, but necessary—as is getting help to address the problem.

Myth 8: If You Work Part-Time, Fewer Days with Longer Hours Is the Best Option

Working three days a week from 8:00 A.M. to 6:00 or 7:00 P.M. and having two full days at home might sound like the best option for a mother returning to work. The truth is that such an arrangement is not better for mothers or for babies, nor is it better for business. John Trougakos, associate professor of organizational behavior and HR management at the University of Toronto-Scarborough, argued that our brains have a limited pool of psychological energy and once that pool is depleted, "we become less effective at everything that we do."[15]

Full-time work is, under the best circumstances, difficult for mothers, but it's certainly not the best situation for a baby who gets her mother already depleted of her emotional energy after a long day at the office and commuting.

It's not that babies can't handle some separation from their mothers; it is natural and healthy for mothers and babies to be sepa-

> It is natural and healthy for mothers and babies to be separated some of the time.

rated some of the time. The issue is the length of that separation and how the baby handles that separation. A short period away each day is better for a young child. This approach allows you time together without long stretches apart.

Most preschools that admit two- or two-and-a-half-year-olds offer only three-hour-long half-day sessions, recognizing that longer separations are too stressful for children at this age. Schools that offer preschool programs for children younger than two are succumbing to pressure from parents for daycare and are more economically rather than psychologically driven.

Myth 9: Quality of Time Is Better Than Quantity of Time

Both quantity and quality time are necessary to raise an emotionally healthy child. But you cannot be emotionally present for your child if you are not physically present as well. Substituting quality time—your undivided attention—for quantity time may seem to be efficient, but it's not really effective.

In an op-ed column that appeared in the *New York Times* on September 5, 2015, Frank Bruni wrote eloquently about the myth of quality time: "There's simply no real substitute for physical presence. . . . We delude ourselves when we say otherwise, when we invoke and venerate 'quality time,' a shopworn phrase with a debatable promise: that we can . . . engineer intimacy at an appointed hour. . . . But people tend not to operate on cue. The surest way to see the brightest colors or the darkest ones is to be watching and waiting and ready for them."[16] When Bruni referred to people, we should remember that *people* includes babies. Bruni noted that more companies have extended family leave for parents, but how many will decide that "the quantity of time with their brood matters as much as the intensity"[17] and be willing to make as much of an investment of hours in their families as their careers is an open question.

Your baby's development—physical, cognitive, and emotional—happens on his time, not your time. You miss more than the physical milestones—the first step, the first word—when you're not with him; you miss essential emotional ones, too. Emotional regulation is a moment-to-moment process. Mothers often have the fantasy that their babies will remain in a state of emotional suspended animation while they are gone, but this is not the case. If your baby is a boat in an ocean of feelings, the ocean may be calm one moment, and stormy the next. Your presence is the ballast that keeps the boat from being rocked too violently or even being swamped.

> Emotional regulation is a moment-to-moment process.

When your baby is in distress or is frightened, he turns to you to soothe and comfort him. It is both your presence and your consistent response that provide him with the security he needs to separate from you in a healthy way. Infants don't understand change. When a baby must rely on an ever-changing array of caregivers or daycare workers, each of whom responds to him in a different way, he may withdraw, or become fearful or aggressive in response to his fear.

When I was growing up, my mother told me that every hour you sleep before midnight is worth three hours after midnight. That may in fact have been her way of getting me to go to sleep, but there is something to be learned from that anecdote. According to the Pew Charitable Research Foundation, the typical working mother spends an average of ninety minutes per day with her child.[18] For most mothers who work outside the home, this time comes at the end of a long day at work, when, let's be honest, we're rarely at our best. When we're tired we have less energy, less patience, and fewer emotional and physical resources to meet the demands of an infant or child who hasn't seen us all day. Your baby can't understand that you had a bad day at work or a lousy commute, that the laundry needs to be done or you need a few minutes for yourself.

For mothers who must work or be away from their babies, the time they *do* spend with their child is very important. There are ways to enhance and maximize the time mother and child spend together (see Chapter 5), but there are occasions, in spite of our best intentions and efforts, when we cannot be present emotionally or give a child what he needs in a limited amount of time. The more time you are able to spend with your child, the more likely it is that you will learn what his needs are and what will best support his developing sense of self and internal emotional security.

Myth 10: The Most Valuable Benefit of Breastfeeding Is Nutrition

When a mother who is away from her child for hours (or days) tells me that her child is getting the best part of breastfeeding because he's getting her milk, I have to disagree. Yes, breastfeeding is important if you can do it. Not only is breast milk the ideal food for infants, but the act of breastfeeding is the most intimate connection you will ever have with another human being. When an infant nurses she has to *work* at sucking and begins to learn to tolerate some frustration, an important developmental milestone—even sucking on the best high-tech engineered artificial nipple isn't the same experience.

The World Health Organization recommends all babies be breastfed for at least one year.[19] Breast milk contains antibodies that protect your baby from illness and lowers his risk of having allergies;

babies breastfed exclusively for the first six months of life have fewer ear infections, respiratory illness, and diarrhea.

But while the nutritional aspect of the breast milk is very important, and preferable to formula, it is *not* the most important part of breastfeeding. A mother who pumps milk for her baby while she's away is giving her child a great gift, but feeding a baby is about the physical *and* emotional experience that he has (and you have), as mothers who do not breastfeed or who have adopted children know.

Physical closeness, whether you breastfeed or bottle feed, is a very important part of nurturing, and physical intimacy is the key ingredient to a good feed for a baby. Many mothers and caregivers don't engage in skin-to-skin contact or make eye contact when they're feeding a baby. Too many are on their cell phones, have the baby turned away from them while holding a bottle to the child's mouth or propping the bottle up so the baby can feed herself. One of the beautiful things about breastfeeding is that it is logistically impossible *not* to face your baby while you're feeding her. Imagine yourself in your baby's place: You lie snugly in your mother's arms, nipple in your mouth, feeling safe and secure. You look longingly into her beautiful eyes while she gives you her full attention, caressing you and holding you next to her warm skin. You hear and feel the reassuring heartbeat that you have known since you lived inside her. As your belly fills with delicious warm milk, you feel deeply satisfied and lulled into a peaceful sleep.

Your baby is getting far more than nutrition when you feed him. Our first experience of love and security is in our mother's arms; your baby is learning how to interact with you from your expression and facial gestures, hearing the tone and melody of your voice, feeling the warmth and texture of your skin; if you or your caregiver props up your baby and feeds him without holding and cuddling him or doesn't make eye contact, then your baby is not getting emotionally what he needs to thrive. This multisensory experience is what helps develop and grow the social emotional part of a baby's brain, not whether you breastfeed or give your baby a bottle.

Myth 11: Cognitive Development Should Be
Encouraged as Early as Possible

Some mothers are competitive about every aspect of their baby's development; they're invested in their child's reaching developmental milestones before everyone else. Dr. Judi Mesman, scientific director of the Institute of Education and Child Studies at Leiden University in Holland, specializes in cross-cultural mothering. Mesman told me she's seen YouTube videos that show parents how to teach their children to roll over; these seem to be uniquely American. Not only will *all* normal babies roll over at some point, but trying to get them to do so before they're interested or ready is neither necessary nor healthy.

In a society that values academic achievement as a barometer of a parents' competence, it's common for parents to worry about their children's cognitive development. Concentrating on your child's cognitive development (left brain) instead of her social emotional development (right brain) before the age of three is like putting on her shoes before her socks. The shoes don't fit, and you wear out the socks.

The first three years of your child's life are a critical window in which to develop your baby's right brain and nurture her emotional health and social development through attachment, play, and nonverbal communication. The development of right-brain attributes, like the ability to read social cues, relate to others, and develop lasting emotional connections, lays the foundation for later cognitive development; without that foundation a child may not be able to tolerate the frustration and mistakes necessary for effective learning or the resilience to recover from making a mistake.

The movement toward play-based, social emotional development in preschool rather than left-brain cognitive development is a significant acknowledgment of the importance of right-brain development. Imagination and creativity are also part of the right-brain function. When parents replace play and personal interaction with screen time like Baby Einstein and flash cards, they interfere with the kind of imaginative and creative play that ultimately helps children work through their fears and difficult feelings like anger and frustration. Thinking a child can read or do math may satisfy a parent's ambition, but a study from New York University's school of education, published in the *Journal of Educational Psychology*, showed that babies who completed the program Your Baby Can Read couldn't, even though their parents thought they could.[20]

This doesn't mean you shouldn't read to your baby and listen to music with her; the most important part of these activities is the social interaction, not the cognitive. Just understand that you're developing her right brain and her emotional intelligence, not her cognitive skills, when you do so. And that's a good thing.

Myth 12: I'll Spoil My Baby If I Hold Her Too Much; She Needs to Learn to Be Independent

Your baby has been inside your body for nine months, floating in a warm bath, never cold, never hungry, the sounds of the outside world muffled, and lulled by the beat of your heart. When she is born, she is not only exposed and vulnerable physically, she lacks, as psychoanalyst Esther Bick said, an emotional "skin" to cope with the stimulation and frustration of the outside world.[21] For the first six months of your baby's life, it is your job as a mother to filter the outside world and protect your baby until she learns how to cope with her new, confusing, and often overwhelming environment.

Spoiled is a judgmental word that is used all too often to refer to babies and children. I believe it is a word that should be used to describe milk that has been unrefrigerated too long, not babies, especially babies under the age of one. Often a mother who has trouble soothing her baby or who doesn't understand what her child needs or who feels frustrated with her child's dependence uses the word *spoiled*. I have found that parents who call their children spoiled or demanding often had the same terms applied to them by their parents. When you feel overwhelmed, it's understandable to want to blame your baby for constantly demanding your time and attention, but what choice does your baby have? If you do not meet your baby's needs, she reacts by behaving in a way—usually crying—to tell you she is uncomfortable or upset.

Humans are biologically and evolutionarily programmed to need their mothers' care until they are almost three years of age. The obstetrical dilemma hypothesis suggests that we are born nine to eleven months too early. One school of thought says it is so our large heads can pass through the birth canal; another more recent school of thought believes that mothers simply do not have enough energy to carry a baby longer than nine months.[22]

Children need as much loving, nurturing, cuddling, comforting, and care as possible in their first three years. A study published in 2009 by researchers at Bar-Ilan University showed that touch reduces cortisol, the stress hormone, in both infants and mothers; the more you hold your baby and respond to your baby's emotional cues, the less stressed he—and you—will be.[23] This confirmed the primate research of Dr. Stephen Suomi, et al., of the National Institute of Child Health and Human Development.[24] Too much cortisol can affect both the immune system and brain development, and not in a good way, and influences long-term health risks for diseases like diabetes and heart disease. Dr. Michael Meaney, a researcher at McGill University, discovered that the more a mother rat licks and grooms her young the fewer stress hormones and the more resilient to stress that baby becomes over its lifetime. According to Meaney, "Secure offspring, regardless of the species, secrete higher levels of growth promoting hormones and lower levels of stress hormones. The emotional health and responsiveness of the mother will determine the health of the offspring."[25]

During her first year, your baby cries because she needs you to provide the things that are necessary to her survival, and she cannot yet comfort herself. That ability is not something a baby is born with—it's something she learns from having her needs met. Crying is the only way she has to communicate what she needs—food, diaper changed, comfort—and she is utterly dependent on others to have those needs met. It is not healthy for your vulnerable infant to cry for long periods of time without being comforted. This is why sleep training in the first six months, before healthy developmental separation has begun, is, in my opinion, too traumatic for babies (and mothers!) and should be postponed until after this most vulnerable period of development.

At around six months, a baby's cries change from desperation when you do not come immediately (*Mommy come right now. I am scared and can't be alone and feel I will die if you don't come*) to dissatisfaction (*You get over here right now and pick me up or I am going to scream until you do, do you hear me?*), which indicates that she may be ready to tolerate slightly greater amounts of frustration. Some babies make this transition later than others, particularly if their mother has not been emotionally available during the first six months.

Dependency and secure attachment are the foundation on which true independence is formed; to become truly independent, your child must spend a long time being dependent. A baby who has learned that she will not have her needs, physical or emotional, met is more likely to become disconnected and have problems creating and maintaining healthy relationships.

Myth 13: Babies Are Born Emotionally Resilient

Allan Schore said, "Babies are not born resilient; they are born malleable."[26] It's an important distinction. Babies are born with varying degrees of adaptability and sensitivity to their surroundings; but no matter what your baby's personality, emotional resilience—the ability to cope with stress and adversity—is created by a constant, loving, comforting, secure presence, ideally that of his mother. (I'll talk more about this in the next chapter.)

The healthy development of the right brain, which controls our resilience to stress throughout life, is a product of the attachment, bonding, and continuous care that a mother provides in the first three years.

Researcher Grazyna Kochanska, at the University of Iowa, discovered that many babies are born with a genetic sensitivity to their environment that makes them more prone to mental illness.[27] These sensitive babies might be the ones who are harder to soothe from birth, the ones who may have greater difficulty connecting with their mothers, or the ones who are perceived to have tummy problems. While all babies have underdeveloped digestive systems for the first two months, some are more prone to what many mothers assume is colic. Colic is digestive, but digestive difficulties are also tied into emotional sensitivity. Sensitivity might also be seen in the babies who seem to have difficulty bonding from the beginning. These babies often have difficulty latching on or seem to have difficulty feeding.

When these babies are in a nurturing environment with a mother who meets their needs for the first three years, their outcome is much better and they have as great a chance to be emotionally healthy as a baby born without this sensitive temperament. However, even the most devoted and present mother cannot always be there to soothe a sensitive baby—and needs some relief—because these babies are often more challenging to care for. An emotionally responsive surrogate caregiver or father can provide support to both mother and baby.

CHAPTER 3

What Does It Mean
to Be a Present Mother?

How Do We Define Presence?

Y ou are sitting on the floor with your one-year-old, close to him but giving him room to play. You make eye contact frequently and lovingly touch him often. You watch him play, cooing and observing and describing his emotions and actions to him. You smile when he smiles at you and wait patiently when he needs to look away or at an object, ready to reengage when he gives you the cues he is ready.

When he is frustrated or angry, you mirror his feelings using your voice and facial expressions. It is helpful to try to imagine your own experience of discovery and wonder as a baby looking at and touching an object for the first time, experiencing it with your own mother. You are enjoying sitting on the floor, playing with your baby and being engaged in the experience, not thinking about the dishes in the sink or your email. You and your baby are involved in a dance of connection and space, attachment and separation, engagement and disengagement, rupture and repair. Sometimes your baby leads and you follow, and sometimes you lead and your baby follows. This playfulness and intimacy help shape your baby's developing brain and personality. To do this you must be in the moment, let go of all the adult means of distraction and stimulation. You need to focus on eye contact, touch, your tone of voice, facial expression, body language, and awareness of your own mood and emotions.

Sometimes you may get bored or sleepy when playing with your baby, feeling understimulated yourself. This is as natural as when your baby looks away for a moment to collect himself and take a break from you. If you wait, then this moment passes and you reengage with your baby.

The Oxford dictionary defines *presence* as "the state or fact of existing, occurring, or being present." Physical presence is the most obvious form of being there; certainly without a mother's physical presence there is no emotional presence for a child. However, it is important to mention that a mother can be with her child physically and still be emotionally checked out.

For a mother to be present, she must first be self-aware of and accept her own (sometimes conflicted) feelings about motherhood. In addition, she must be willing to make her child a priority in the time she spends with her. This means not only spending as much time as possible with a child during her first three years of life but also focusing on how that time is spent. We're addicted to multitasking—reading our email while watching TV, sneaking a peek at our text messages at the dinner table. Yet researchers like Earl Miller, a neuroscientist at MIT, have shown that, in fact, that kind of divided attention is both destructive to relationships and stressful to individuals.[1]

Presence also means emotional engagement. Dr. Beatrice Beebe, of Columbia University, and Dr. Miriam Steele, of the New School for Social Research, have done a lot of research in attachment and infant–mother interaction. They described in great detail the impor_tance of the attunement of a mother to a baby in the early years. At_tunement is another way of describing the dance of emotional interaction between a baby and a mother.[2] When we dance, we need a partner who is present, responsive, and interactive, or else we are es_sentially dancing alone. This dance is how a mother helps her child learn to negotiate relationships and to develop a secure sense of herself in the world.

Presence means finding enjoyment in the experience of being with your baby and being able to tolerate the boring moments. Discovering the beauty and fascination in the little things throughout the day that your baby is learning. Presence means pleasure.

Fiona worked as a sales rep for a china manufacturer. After the birth of her first child she decided not to return to work, with the full support of her husband and her mother, who had stayed home until Fiona was in the third grade, and then went back to work part-time. Fiona had loved being pregnant and nursing and recognized that being able to be with her four children when they were very young was a privilege. She said, wryly, if "someone messed them up I would rather it be me than a stranger." Fiona relished every developmental step forward her children made, no matter how small.

"I loved being home so I could be in the moment with my children, sitting on the floor; I loved seeing something new in their eyes or watching them follow the dog. . . . I would talk to them so I felt connected to them. It may not have been like having an intellectual conversation with them, but there was something else going on that I found equally as fascinating in every little gesture."

Finally, presence means that when a mother cannot be there, she is sensitive to the cues of her child when she returns, she is aware when she has been away too long or is too disconnected. Children are wise beyond their years. They are born with an innate sense of their essential needs and a pace of development that is unique to each of them. The co-director of the New School's Attachment Research Center, Dr. Howard Steele, quotes Mary Ainsworth in defining *sensitive mothering* as the capacity to respond promptly with appropriate care and concern to a child's distress.[3] When a mother is present for her child, she learns to read and interpret her child's subtle (and sometimes not so subtle) nonverbal cues, which will tell her what that child needs and how he is coping with separation. A mother's sensitivity will alert her to whether those needs are being met, or not, and can instruct her in how to help her baby upon her return. For example, when a baby is extremely anxious and clingy, or turns away from his mother after a separation, a sensitive mother recognizes this as her child's experience that she has been gone too long, and she needs to repair the rift.

We do not live in a perfect world, and there are times when we cannot meet all of our children's needs emotionally or physically. When this happens, we need to know how to repair the misalignment of their needs and our ability to meet those needs. You have to accept that some of these failures can be healed and some cannot. Repairing the separation makes a baby emotionally stronger and more resilient; immediately addressing the damage created by absence and temporary disconnection is the most successful approach to repairing it, but it is never too late to do so, even with adult children. I will address how mothers can learn to repair these misalignments in Chapter 8.

Why Are Mothers Uniquely Important?

In this book I've focused on mothers' physical and emotional presence, not that of fathers or caregivers. As a psychoanalyst, I have always recognized the importance of mothers as primary nurturers. A mother's role is specific and not interchangeable with the roles of other caregivers—no matter how loving, valuable, or necessary.

Our denial of the very specific and special physical and emotional role of a mother to her child, particularly in our attempt to be modern, is not in the best interest of children and their needs. Babies depend in every way on their mothers for food, comfort, reassurance, and the ability to manage an overwhelming, overstimulating world of internal and environmental sensations. Mothers help very young children—from newborns to three-year-olds—feel that their presence in this world is valuable. Mothers serve a critical function for a newborn; they are what Myron A. Hofer, of Columbia University, called the psycho-biological regulators of the baby's environment.[4] Like a mother bird feeding its young, human mothers "digest" strong emotions and experiences for their babies and help them begin to learn how to cope by making sure that their emotions are neither too high nor too low.

Today, when fathers are more involved in raising their children than ever before, the idea of the unique and irreplaceable role of a mother may seem old-fashioned. And yet there is significant evidence that biology has an impact on the different ways men and women nurture, and the most recent research has shown that a mother's unique presence is critical to the emotional development and mental health of her children in their early years.

Hormonal Research and the Uniqueness of Mothers

Researchers at the National Institute of Mental Health, including Dr. Tom Insel, have identified traits of sensitive mothering and protectiveness connected to the hormones oxytocin and vasopressin, respectively.[5] While both genders produce both hormones, females produce more oxytocin, and males produce more vasopressin. Because of this biological difference, women and men are unique in their roles as parents, different but both important.

> Women and men are unique in their roles as parents, different but both important.

Oxytocin is called the trust or bonding hormone; it helps create and strengthen a unique bond between a mother and child, and to a lesser degree, a father and child. Vasopressin is responsible for the aggressively protective response you might see in a mother or father when their baby is threatened.

Oxytocin is produced when a mother gives birth and breastfeeds, but also when she is emotionally present with her baby. In humans this means touching, gazing, reflecting, and comforting. Larry Young, a neuroscientist at the Emory University School of Medicine, noted: "Oxytocin receptors are highly concentrated in areas of the brain involved in visual attention, eye gaze, and some auditory (hearing) attention. It's the eye contact and the face to face connection that helps build that bond." In addition, Insel found oxytocin was critical for the development of trust, empathy, face memory, and generosity.[6] The more a mother engages with her baby, the more oxytocin she produces; the more oxytocin she produces, the more she bonds with her child; in other words, the more you love your baby, the more you can love your baby.

The adage "Use it or lose it" holds true in regard to oxytocin.

Insel's research with voles showed how sensitive mothering is passed down from generation to generation;[7] Young's research reinforced this.[8] Insel found that voles were born with a finite number of oxytocin receptors, which were activated by the nurturing of their mothers. The offspring of mothers who were not well nurtured not only produced less oxytocin but also had fewer activated oxytocin receptors in their brains; with fewer receptors, they also experienced fewer positive effects of oxytocin.[9]

Dr. James Rilling, of Emory University, has done extensive research on how hormones affect the mother–child bond in humans, the important role oxytocin plays in a mother's ability to nurture and connect with her baby, and the biological differences between female and male styles of nurturing. He found hormones like estrogen and prolactin promote oxytocin receptors that usually make "the mother bond [to her child] right away."[10] Rilling also found that elevated levels of testosterone reduce oxytocin. This may explain why the higher the testosterone, the greater the investment in mating, but the lower the investment in nurturing.[11]

I believe this may be the explanation of why men who are very aggressive or seem to have traits linked to testosterone seem to have less ability to be empathic. It may also suggest that though fathers can be "good enough" caregivers, it is not biologically natural to most men to provide the degree of empathetic care that comes more instinctively to most women. For example, when a toddler falls down and hurts himself, the response of most mothers is to immediately show concern and try to comfort the child. A more typical father's response is to encourage or tell the child that he is fine and he should pick himself up and get on with things. This does not mean that fathers are not loving or that their unique style of nurturing and protection is not important to a child's well-being; they are. If a child is fleeing from a predator or other danger, he needs to be able to get on his feet quickly if he falls.

Later in a child's life, the male style of nurturing helps a child create a healthy separation from his mother and explore the world on his own.

Research on oxytocin by Dr. Ruth Feldman, at Bar Ilan University in Israel, showed the very real biological differences between men and women in terms of nurturing. Feldman observed that fathers normally displayed less touching, gazing, and empathic behaviors than mothers. But when they were given oxytocin via a nasal spray, fathers touched their babies and looked into their eyes more; they showed more sensitive parental behavior overall, but their behavior was still more playful and stimulating than it was calming. Not only does Feldman's research clearly demonstrate the biological differences between the way women and men nurture children, it also offers ways to improve parenting skills to people in diverse family structures.[12] For instance, in the future, a single father, or a two-father family may be prescribed intranasal oxytocin to improve their sensitive nurturing. These findings also encourage more research on how we can teach fathers to be more sensitive nurturers.

Dr. Tracy Bale, a researcher from the University of Pennsylvania, studies the differences between male and female brains. Bale's research into the role of corticosterone production and stress on a fetus in utero, and how it may impact the developing male brain differently from the way it affects the female brain, may eventually answer why there is a higher rate of autism in boys than girls.[13] "The type of stress that is specific to prenatal and postnatal periods is different because the brain is developing and maturing very differently before and after birth." Her research may also have implications about how much stress women should be exposed to in the workplace and the best time to begin maternity leave for the health of both mother and child.

Right-Brain Development and Emotional Health

New technologies have enabled researchers to prove what attachment researchers and psychoanalysts have known for decades: A mother's presence and attachment to her baby in the first three years of life are critical for the development of the social part of the baby's brain and for the ability of the baby to cope with stress. Cutting-edge neuro-imaging technology allows us to observe and document the relationship between brain development and human interaction, letting us capture real-time dynamics of the brain. The use of functional magnetic resonance imaging (fMRI) and near infrared spectroscopy (NIRS) has permitted researchers to see brain development, blood flow, and brain activity, giving them the opportunity to understand more fully the connection between the brain's emotionally centered right hemisphere and its stress-regulating parts (the limbic system, including the hypothalamus, amygdala, and hippocampus). Recent research from the Washington University School of Medicine in St. Louis showed that the brains of preschool children who had nurturing mothers had a larger hippocampus, a brain structure involved in learning, memory, and emotional regulation. Joan Luby, a child psychiatrist at St. Louis Children's Hospital, said the "study suggests there's a sensitive period when the brain responds more to maternal support."[14]

Dr. Nim Tottenham at UCLA demonstrated that the brain has "sensitive periods of development," which are critical for the social part of the baby's brain, and, in her words, "essential in the shaping of the neural architecture of the amygdala [the part of the brain that helps regulate our emotions and responds to fear] and its connections to the prefrontal cortex [the gray matter, which plays a large role in personality development]. . . . There are early moments in development when events can exert lasting and potent effects on future behavior."[15] It is during these sensitive periods in the first thousand days of life that the nurturing environment plays an essential role in providing the foundation for brain plasticity—the brain's ability to change its own structure in response to changes in the body or the environment—throughout life, including the capacity to learn.

This complex but essential part of the early developing brain is responsible not only for emotional regulation and resilience to stress but also for nonverbal communication of all kinds, including empathic responses and the ability to read social cues and to connect deeply with others on an emotional level.

Allan Schore, who has focused his entire career on the importance of attachment and right-brain development, stated, "The right brain is the part of the brain where feelings reside and get processed including the processing of new information." According to Schore, the right brain is the home of "nonverbal, unconscious, holistic and subjective emotional information processing, as well as . . . the highest human functions of stress regulation, inter-subjectivity, humor, empathy, compassion, morality, and creativity."[16]

We would like to believe that our children are "just fine" when we leave them, so we can hurry back to our careers and social lives as quickly as possible. The truth is not always this simple. In an article published in the *Journal of Child Psychology and Psychiatry*, researchers James F. Leckman and J. S. March were emphatic on this point: "All children are not 'resilient' and there is now compelling evidence that adverse developmental and biological disruptions occurring in the early years of life are rapidly increasing, as is their consequences in the declining mental health of our children."[17] As we struggle to explain the increase in the numbers of children diagnosed with conditions on the autism spectrum, ADHD, and other social and developmental disorders, we have to consider that this rise may be directly related to increased maternal stress and the lack of consistent, intimate engagement of mothers (and other caregivers) with children.

Sensitive Nurturing and Resilience to Stress

In the first three years of life, it is the interaction of child and mother or other caregiver that establishes the child's patterns of response to people and her environment, as well as her individual capacity to cope with environmental stress. A mother's sensitive nurturing and presence in those years is a powerful influence on a child's ability to stabilize her emotions and her ability to cope with stressful events and feelings throughout life. This early relationship creates the foundation for a lifetime of emotional health and stability.

A mother's boredom with her nurturing role and/or her depression, disengagement, or absence can all lead to a disruption in a baby's development. I tell my patients that boredom is remembering the feeling of your mother being bored with you. Because their mothers struggled with the demands of nurturing, these women often struggle more with mothering their own children.

> Boredom is remembering the feeling of your mother being bored with you.

According to Dr. Andrew Garner, co-author of the American Academy of Pediatrics' "Policy Statement and Technical Report on Toxic Stress," "Toxic stress reflects an inability to turn off the body's stress response. Toxic stress happens in the absence of resilience. Resilience is the ability to adapt to adversity in a healthy manner. The buffer for toxic stress is engaged nurturing."[18] Engaged nurturing requires a calm, reflective, and responsive mother.

Garner also noted that early adversity such as neglect, maternal depression, or the lack of a secure attachment may produce a lasting and chronic stress response, which alters the brain's ability to cope with stress in the future. It may also produce symptoms like ADHD or anxiety or feelings of restlessness. This kind of a stress response in young children can lead to less visible yet permanent changes in brain structure and function.[19]

Research has shown that a baby's developing limbic system—the part of the brain that controls the autonomic nervous system and regulates our stress response—is positively shaped by sensitive parenting and maternal presence and that early stressful experiences or social adversity can, as Nim Tottenham said, "increase the risk for psychopathology [mental or emotional illness]."[20] According to Young, this is the result of a negative feedback loop in which stress promotes the production of a specific stress hormone, which in turn suppresses the release of oxytocin. However, the release of oxytocin in the baby's brain, which is promoted by nurturing, protects the brain from the negative effects of stressful events.[21]

Can Sensitive Nurturing Protect Against Mental Illness and Developmental Disorders? The Role of Epigenetics

Humans are a combination of hormones and early experiences, wrote Tom Insel and Michael Numan in their book, *The Neurobiology of Parental Behavior*.[22] Epigenetics is the study of how the environment can affect the way our DNA functions, or expresses itself. For example, if you have a family history of skin cancer, you are more likely to develop skin cancer too. However, if you limit your sun exposure and always wear sunscreen, you dramatically improve your chances of avoiding skin cancer. There is also growing evidence that stress and trauma impact our DNA. When a baby has a sensitive and present mother, the outcome for that baby in terms of brain development and DNA expression is likely to be different from that for a child who has an absent or distracted mother.

In an article in the *Journal of Child Psychology and Psychiatry* titled "Developmental Neuroscience Comes of Age," Dr. James Leckman wrote that the "relations between a child and caregiver within the first years of life can have direct and enduring effects on the child's brain development and behavior. . . . The enduring impact of early maternal care and the role of epigenetic modifications of the genome during critical periods in early brain development in health and disease is likely to be one of the most important discoveries in all of science that have major implications for our field."[23]

Dr. Steve Cole, who studies the impact of environment on gene expression at the University of California, Los Angeles, said,

> Kids need a sense of security and a sense of trust in others who take care of them. Early life experiences structure the developmental trajectories of our gene expression systems. In the absence of a sense of social security and trust, our bodies are programmed to mortgage our future health to maximize short-term survival. If you believe the world is a threatening or unsafe place, the body is programmed to activate inflammatory genes to defend against infection and help with wound healing in the present, but long-term inflammation becomes fuel for chronic illness; it is not just somatic [physical] disease risk that emerges but psychological risk too, because inflammatory signals can promote depression and anxiety.[24]

Research by Drs. Grazyna Kochanska, Robert A. Philibert, and Robin A. Barry, from the University of Iowa, has shown sensitive and consistent maternal nurturing can change the outcome for a child who has a genetic predisposition for mental health issues. According to the researchers, many children are born with a short allele (an allele is one of a pair of genes that appears at a particular place on a particular chromosome and controls the same characteristic) on their serotonin receptor, which affects their ability to feel pleasure and cope with stress.[25]

The emotions of these sensitive children are closer to the surface and their reactions are more intense; they may be more sensitive to noise and overstimulation as well as understimulation. They are less easily soothed and may be labeled as having colic when they are infants and called "difficult" as toddlers, as they may be prone to tantrums or inconsolable distress. These children may have as good a chance of growing up emotionally healthy as a child without this genetic profile if they receive sensitive maternal nurturing in their early years.

Unlike Bruno Bettelheim's theory of the "refrigerator mother," which attributes a child's autism or social developmental issues solely to a mother's lack of warmth and affection,[26] today we understand that autistic-like symptoms may be a combination of genetics and environment. Children may have a genetic predisposition that is affected by prenatal stress and/or the lack of engagement or interaction of their primary caregivers. With our increased understanding of the influence of the environment on gene expression we can see the delicate balance of nature *and* nurture, but with a strong emphasis on nurture.

Mothers and Emotional Security

Like other animals, babies use sound, touch, and smell as primal ways to distinguish their mothers from other caregivers, including their fathers. There have been a number of studies that document just how accurately babies recognize the uniqueness of their mothers. In research by Drs. Jennifer M. Cernoch and Richard H. Porter of Vanderbilt University, babies who were presented with a breast pad soaked with their mother's milk on one side and one with a stranger's milk on the other side turn their heads toward their mother's very specific smell. Babies will also turn toward their mother's voice, which they have heard since they were in utero, and away from the voice of another caregiver.[27]

Children will always choose their mothers over a substitute unless that mother has turned away from nurturing and rejected mothering. Early in my professional life, I worked as a social worker in a clinic that served families from a variety of socioeconomic backgrounds. There I saw many foster children who, unfortunately, had been taken from their parents because they had been abused and physically neglected. What shocked me was that time and time again children who had been repeatedly abused by their parents still wanted to return to them. No matter how caring and loving the foster parents were toward these children, they still craved the physical and emotional presence of their birth parents over substitutes.

Does this mean that adoptive parents, foster parents, fathers, and nannies cannot be sensitive caregivers? Of course not! And if a mother is truly unable (for whatever reason) to nurture her child, it is better to have another consistent primary loving caregiver in the child's life.

Yet we also know that having an emotionally healthy and present mother is the ideal situation. If you need proof that the pull of the biological mother and child is strong, look at the number of adopted children who seek out their birth mothers, even when they have been raised in a loving family. You could say that this instinctual yearning to connect with our biology (kinship bonds) is part of what has helped humans survive. It is, perhaps, one of the reasons grandparents have such a special bond with their grandchildren, and grandmothers and aunts have, historically, been so intimately involved in caring for their relatives' children.

Humans are the only mammals that are born very dependent and remain so for a long time. In fact, there are some scientists, like Karen Rosenberg and Wenda Trevathan, who believe that humans give birth too early for ideal brain and physical development and that babies should gestate for eighteen to twenty-two months.[28] The obstetrical dilemma hypothesis is an anthropological theory that posits our bigger brains (in relation to our size) forced humans to give birth sooner after conception to allow the baby's head to fit through the mother's birth canal. As a result, human babies are far more fragile and dependent on their mothers for a longer time than many other mammals. It is our infants' helplessness that makes bonding to one primary caregiver an evolutionary and biological necessity.

A mother's overall physical and emotional presence increases the chances of a child internalizing a sense of security, which will follow him throughout life. If his mother is not with him in the first months of his life, the child feels she has ceased to exist; in psychoanalytic terms, the baby has not developed a sense of object constancy. We now know that an infant is aware that his mother is not present shortly after birth. At around eight months of age a mother will see a more dramatic difference in her baby's anxiety over her comings and goings; we call this separation anxiety. During this period—from eight to eighteen months—a baby becomes more aware that his mother is separate from him and begins to understand that his mother can leave and not return. When a mother goes to work or runs to the supermarket, an infant or toddler experiences her absence as a loss; he feels her absence as permanent. If, when she returns, she can acknowledge her child's sad and angry feelings and is willing to accept any guilt she feels about leaving her child (even if she needed and enjoyed the time away from him), she can repair the feelings of loss caused by her absence.

When an infant or toddler cries and no one responds to his distress and there is no mother to comfort him, he almost immediately experiences this as a social adversity or loss. Studies by attachment researcher Dr. Mary Ainsworth found that out of twenty-three crying infants, those whose mothers responded to their cries and comforted them were better able to soothe themselves after their first year than those who were left to cry and whose mother's physical presence was denied them.[29]

How many times have you seen a baby suck her thumb to comfort herself when her mother has left the room? Or a toddler reach for a teddy bear or blanket to comfort himself when he must separate from his mother to go to sleep? All babies can tolerate small amounts of frustration, and their ability to tolerate frustration increases with time and age if they do not have to separate *too early, for too long,* and *chronically* from their mothers, who are their source of security.

A small amount of frustration can help a child develop the internal resources to be able to soothe himself, and no developmental psychologist or psychoanalyst will tell you that you should try to prevent all frustration. But the capacity of a four-month-old to cope with a mother's absence is very different from the coping ability of a three-year-old toddler. An infant's developing brain is overwhelmed by the feelings of grief at the perceived loss of his mother and often copes by rejecting (even temporarily) or turning away from his mother or by becoming extremely anxious, fearful, and clingy.

The older toddler has the mental and emotional capacity not just to feel the loss of his mother, but to forgive her and allow her to help him repair the loss. It is not until a child is approximately eighteen months old that he can hold the image of his mother in his mind and can even start to make sense of his mother's physical absence. If, by that time, an infant has had what pediatrician, psychoanalyst, and child development researcher Donald Winnicott called a "good enough" experience of his mother[30]—that is, a mother who is present enough of the time, does not deny that her absence causes her baby pain, and takes steps to repair the loss as quickly as possible—then the child will internalize and hold on to the reassuring, soothing presence of his mother and can wait for longer periods of time without panicking until she returns. This is the beginning of ego development, the development of a strong sense of security and self. It is this foundation that helps a child become more resilient to stress in the future, more independent in a healthy way to regulate his moods and emotions throughout life.

If a mother's presence is so important during this attachment period, what happens when a mother is away for much of the day, either at work or engaged in other activities? Children develop a variety of healthy defenses when they are apart from their mothers or need emotional space when they are with their mothers. The word *defense* means "to protect," and there are some defenses that are healthy and protect a child from real or perceived threats. These include self-soothing mechanisms like sucking their thumb or focusing their attention on something other than their mother. There are, however, unhealthy or maladaptive defenses that children develop to deal with pain, which either interrupt or interfere with that child's emotional development. These include premature independence, extreme aggression, consistent emotional disengagement, and clinginess. When you leave your three-year-old at nursery school for the first time, it's normal for him to be a little aggressive or shy while he tries to figure out how to negotiate the new environment, and it's normal for this behavior to last for several days, or even a few weeks, until he's comfortable with the new situation. If the behavior persists, and prevents him from making friends and integrating into the class, it is considered a maladaptive defense.

In 2003 the Commission on Children at Risk produced a report titled *Hardwired to Connect.* Thirty-three pediatricians, researchers, and mental health professionals concluded: "The declining mental health of many US children is a pressing issue that plays a substantial role in many of today's emerging physical problems, psychosomatic and psychosocial disorders and has pronounced and long lasting effects on both children's lives and society."[31] This increase in the incidence of mental illness in children is, I believe, connected to the increasing disinterest in and devaluing of mothering in our society.

When Jane met with me, she was clearly distraught. She had come to talk about Roger, her three-year-old son and only child. The head of his preschool had called again about Roger's behavior—he was having difficulty paying attention to the teacher's instructions. His teacher was obviously concerned that Roger seemed to be constantly distracted in class and disrupted quiet time for the other children. Jane was worried, and annoyed that she had to take time from her demanding job as a marketing executive to deal with these issues. She didn't understand why her son was behaving this way and was angry that the principal felt that Roger needed therapy, or possibly even medication. She didn't understand what she had done wrong. She and her husband had bought a home in a family-friendly neighborhood, Roger's room was stocked with toys and stuffed animals, and he had a competent, responsible nanny (though not as affectionate and interactive as Jane might have liked). Jane always made an effort to be home by 6:30 to spend time with her son every evening before he went to bed at 7:30, and, of course, they were together on the weekends. After a little prodding from me, Jane admitted that yes, she did spend some of her "alone time" with her son on the computer catching up on work or on the phone with her friends. And sometimes she was simply too tired to play with Roger and often let him watch TV or a movie, or play with her iPad so she could have some time to herself.

Jane made changes to their daily routine and how she spent her time with her son (see Chapter 5 for some of the techniques she used to help Roger deal with her absence). Through our work together, I was able to help Jane see that her challenges being with Roger were connected to her early experiences of feeling that her own mother was preoccupied and emotionally absent. Jane had not felt like a priority to her mother, who, though she had taken care of her daughter's basic needs, had rarely shown she enjoyed her company or played with her. Jane decided it was important to spend more time with Roger in a more focused and less distracted way. She scaled back her hours at the office and came home earlier so she could spend more time with her son. She put away her cell phone and tablet, and learned to relax with Roger. She sat on the floor with her son, and let him direct her. By allowing herself to engage with him in a slower, quieter way, she became his playmate. It was less tiring to her and more satisfying to Roger.

Jane and Roger are a success story. Jane found ways to spend more time with Roger, and she changed the way she spent time with him; this created a change in and softening of Roger's behavior. All too often I see parents after their child has been diagnosed with a behavioral, social, or attention disorder, and then the damage is much harder—though not impossible—to repair. I feel there is always hope for families if parents are willing to look at their own behaviors as well as those of their children.

> There is always hope for families if parents are willing to look at their own behaviors as well as those of their children.

Researcher Dr. Suniya Luthar, at Columbia University, found that children born to wealthy or upper-middle-class parents experienced similar emotional difficulties and mental illnesses as children born into severely socioeconomically deprived families; children born to parents who were in the socioeconomic middle seemed to do the best.[32] What do families at either socioeconomic extreme—both wealthy and poor—have in common? The mothers are often absent, both physically and emotionally. A poor mother who suffers from extreme social adversity is more likely to be depressed, concerned with day-to-day survival, and have little flexibility in the kind of work she does and the hours she works. A wealthy mother, or one who has chosen a profession that demands most of her time and attention, may put her social or professional commitments and material needs ahead of spending time with her children and may outsource much of the childcare to others because she has the resources to do so. Parents in the middle are more likely to get home earlier from work, to not have the kind of work that preoccupies them at home, and to tend to focus on relationships rather than material success.

We have a values dilemma in the United States. We focus on giving our children (and ourselves) things rather than our time, attention, and engagement. We don't want to recognize that raising healthy children requires putting their needs ahead of our own for a time. We want to do everything quickly. We want to eat quickly, run quickly, talk quickly, and we want our children to separate from us quickly. We are so impatient to return to our "real" lives, the one before our children, that we often sacrifice our kids' emotional and mental health in the process of rushing back.

Inga is a fifty-year-old Danish mother of two teenage sons. A freelance artist, she worked from her studio at home. When I interviewed her for this book she expressed her joy of mothering when her boys were infants and toddlers. She spoke about how it seems to her that Americans have trouble appreciating slowness and seem to need so much action and constant stimulation. She compared being with a baby to watching the subtlety of the seasons changing. It is beautiful and exciting and stimulating, but if you are expecting an action film you will be disappointed.

Our desire to speed up our separation from our children and make them independent of us suits our own needs to go back to work, or to socialize, or get back to our lives. Just as we now understand that it is best for the emotional health of an infant to let the baby's hunger determine when she should be fed, rather than feeding her when it suits us, we now understand that our child's ability to separate from us in a healthy way is best determined by the baby and her time clock, not ours; to do so too early may create developmental issues for the child.

When Mothers Are Physically Present but Emotionally Absent

What happens when mothers are physically present but emotionally absent? When a mother is distracted, depressed, or conflicted about motherhood or preoccupied with other things, whether it's household tasks, outside work, or social activities, a child experiences this withdrawal of her mother's attention as a loss. A baby whose mother ignores or is not attentive to her emotional needs may turn away from her mother as a defense or may become very clingy and aggressive in her need for attention. Take Mary, for example.

Mary worked full time as a lawyer at a big-city law firm before she had her daughter, Ariel, and then a son, Timothy, two years later. After Ariel was born she decided to be a stay-at-home mother. She had a full-time babysitter and although Mary was very competent at organizing her children's activities, she found it hard to spend extended time with her three-year-old daughter or one-year-old son. She became bored if she had to be with them for too long. She retreated to text messaging, to frequent visits to the gym, or to lunches with friends. Mary came to see me because Ariel was very aggressive at home with her brother and with her peers at school. Mary was worried about her daughter and her difficulty feeling deeply connected to her. She wanted to understand why, even though she stayed at home and gave up her work to be a mother, she failed to give her daughter what she needed.

Although Mary gave up her work outside the home to "stay home with her children," she was bored and uncomfortable with the emotional demands of nurturing them. Mary yearned for the distraction and adult interaction of her legal career and used every opportunity to separate from her son and daughter. Not only was she not present physically much more than a mother who works full time out of the home but she found it difficult to interact or remain connected to her children consistently when she was with them.

Mothers often ask me, "When is it okay to go back to work? When can I have a life again outside my baby's needs?" I never respond to this question lightly, but I do believe that the first three years of life are critical to a child's development and personality formation. If a mother who has the option of working can sacrifice some of her ambition and make her child her priority, she and he will reap the benefits in the long run. As your child, grows, he will interpret the world based on the tools you have given him. He will need you in a less intense way, but he will still need you.

In my work with Mary, we were able to distinguish her desire to go back to work, for more adult company and intellectual stim-

ulation—which was a real desire—from the boredom and disconnection she felt being with her children. She became aware
that she was afraid of her children's dependence on her because
she did not want to deal with her own unmet need to be taken
care of. In therapy she was able to mourn her own lost feelings
of vulnerability and face the fear that no one would care for her.
Mary went back to work part-time, and when she was with her
children she was able to be present and engaged with them.

I am not saying that mothers can, or should, be present and tuned
into a child's needs every minute. In addition to this being impossible
physically and emotionally for a mother, it would be terrible for the
child. A child *needs* to experience some frustration of her mother not
meeting all of her needs. In fact, most children are fairly tolerant of
their mother's imperfections. The children who suffer the most are
those whose mothers are not aware of or do not pay attention to the
signs their child gives them that they were absent for too long. Self-
awareness is the key to balancing your
needs with those of your child. Your child
will let you know when she is ready to be
more separate and more independent and
can tolerate your absence; her development will progress on her timetable, not
yours. Presence is not perfection. Presence
is what some researchers have called "right
brain to right brain communication."
Many studies have shown that the physical interaction—gaze and
touch—as well as the emotional attunement of mother and baby are
essential to the development of the right brain of an infant.[33] The capacity to develop in a healthy manner, to regulate stress, to balance
emotions, and to feel for another human being begins with mothers.

> Self-awareness is
> the key to balancing
> your needs with
> those of your child.

What Do Attachment and Emotional Security Have to Do with Presence?

Simply put, attachment is the emotional bond that forms between an infant and her primary caregiver, ideally her mother. It is not just how a child gets her primary needs met—food, safety, comfort in times of distress, emotional regulation, and the feeling that she is not alone—it also forms the basis for her later social, emotional, and cognitive development. I may need to get a little technical here, but bear with me. It's important.

Attachment and Emotional Security

Attachment is the building block for the development of the self, essential for good self-esteem in a child and necessary for her survival. The word *secure* is used to describe an individual child's trust that her mother will be responsive to her when she is in need.

According to John Bowlby, the father of attachment theory, "the point of attachment is to maintain proximity between a child and mother to promote the protection and survival of the child. When the child is confident of his mother as a secure and safe base he is free to explore the environment. The sensitive responsiveness of his mother determines the quality of the attachment bond and the beliefs about what to expect from relationships and from himself."[34] Attachment is responsible for building "internal working models" that allow us to imagine interactions and conversations with others based on our previous experiences with them. In the first three years of his life, a child is, according to Bowlby, busy "constructing working models of how the physical world may be expected to behave, how his mother and other significant persons may be expected to behave, how he himself may be expected to behave, and how each interacts with the other."[35] In addition, "A child builds his secure sense of self on how confident he feels that his attachment figures are readily available or whether he is more or less afraid that they will not be available—occasionally, frequently or most of the time."[36] A securely attached child has had the benefit of a consistently responsive mother. A child whose emotional needs are ignored or otherwise not met is more likely to be insecure and may become defensively independent to avoid being hurt or disappointed, both as a child and as an adult.

It is through this attachment to his mother that a child develops his beliefs about whether others can be trusted to be caring and loving and whether he is valuable and worthy of being cared for. It is important that a baby be able to depend on his mother and can express that need. Dependency is an essential bridge to healthy separation and critical for intimate love. This "internal working model" is a baby's model for all relationships in the future.[37]

It is normal for a securely attached baby to react when she is separated from her mother. It is of equal importance that a baby can expect her mother will comfort her when she is distressed. A securely attached baby can balance the need for her mother to help regulate her emotions or comfort her with her ability to comfort herself, particularly when her mother is not present. Secure attachment is also related to a child's ability to express distress or negative emotions without fear that she will be ignored or punished. That is, a child whose mother is for the most part continuously sensitive to her needs and is available emotionally can have small and occasional lapses in how she responds to her child.

Attachment First, Separation Next

Strong attachment makes healthy separation easier. If your mooring is secure, you can leave your boat knowing that it will be there when you return. If you feel your mooring might move or disappear, then you would be afraid to leave your boat, fearing that it might not be there later, leaving you stranded. If we want our children to be able to relate to others and have healthy relationships, to be interdependent, they need to be able to be dependent first.

Our fears in infancy of being separated from our mother are based on the very real possibility that if our mother does not care for us we could die. From birth to around three months, an infant has no boundaries; she does not distinguish between where she ends and her mother begins. You could think of this state as a continuation of being in her mother's womb, and sometimes the first three months of a child's life is called the fourth trimester. Because human babies are completely dependent on their mothers for so long after birth, this blurring of physical boundaries is necessary for a child's survival. By three months, a baby has started to learn the dance of needing, crying, and being responded to by her mother. This is the beginning of the recognition that her mother is a separate being.

Somewhere between six and eight months, if a baby's mother is physically and emotionally present enough, she develops a moderate fear of being separated from her, or separation anxiety. This is a normal and necessary part of development and is the transition to a child's practicing independence and feeling emotionally secure. Separation anxiety is the realization that Mom can leave and not come back, and because babies at this age live in the present with little recognition of the future, they are afraid that when Mom is gone, she is really gone and she may never see her again. In a securely attached child, this fear subsides around eighteen months.

At this point a baby begins to practice deliberately separating herself from her mother, or what attachment researcher Dr. Margaret Mahler calls rapprochement.[38] If you've ever watched a toddler playing or exploring independently, he will "touch base" with his mother, either literally, by coming over and touching or holding on to her briefly, or figuratively, through eye contact. It is this back and forth between mother and toddler that gives a child the sense that he can handle new experiences. This period of exploration and reconnection goes more smoothly when babies feel securely attached. Classic children's books like Margaret Wise Brown's *The Runaway Bunny* and *Goodnight Moon* depict excellent examples of the push and pull of toddler separation. These books are enduringly beloved. In *The Runaway Bunny*, a baby bunny tests his desire to explore and separate from his mother as well as his mother's unconditional love and acceptance. When the mother bunny follows her baby, as mothers do when their toddlers storm off and slam the door to their room, she proves that he can explore the world and she will always be there for him, no matter what, as a touchstone of security. In *Goodnight Moon*, the mother spends a great deal of time helping her child make the transition to sleep by saying good night to every toy, creature, and object in the room, taking time to assure the child she is secure before slipping into slumber, which is one of the scariest transitions for a child.

Your child's ability to be separate from you is important; it is, in fact, as important as her secure attachment to you. But your baby needs to learn to be separate and practice independence at her own pace, and that process will go more smoothly if she is securely attached. If you've observed toddlers and babies in a playground or play space, you've seen a child play by herself or with another child, look for her mother or come over to her briefly, then go back to playing. With her mother present, that child is also more likely to explore and take social risks, like approaching another child or climbing on a piece of playground equipment farther away from her mother.

We know from Jay Belsky's extensive research that children who are in nonmaternal care or who are away from their primary caregiver and are put into daycare *early* (under the age of one), who spend *extensive* time (full or near full time) in daycare, and who are in daycare consistently until the start of preschool at age three are at higher risk of aggressive behavior and emotional problems than those who spend fewer hours a week in nonmaternal or non-primary-caregiver care. Belsky's earlier research also showed that children who spent less than twenty hours a week in daycare did best.[39]

When a mother tells me how she encourages her baby to be independent, I'm concerned. A baby who is learning independence on his mother's schedule, not his own, may be learning that he cannot depend on the most important person in his life at a vulnerable time and may become disconnected emotionally. Sleep training à la Ferber, multiple short-term caregivers, and long separations without immediate repair (see more on this in Chapter 5) are some of the things that can trip up a child's tentative steps toward healthy independence.

Attachment Difficulties

Mary Ainsworth, who is considered one of the matriarchs of attachment research, found there were three types of attachment: secure, insecure avoidant, and insecure ambivalent.[40] Mary Main, a prominent attachment researcher, later identified a fourth type, insecure disorganized, and also identified the attachment styles in infancy that corresponded to emotional security or pathology in the future.[41]

Ainsworth created what is now known as the Strange Situation Experiment, a series of separations and reunions between mothers and one-year-old babies.[42] First a mother and baby enter a room, and the mother plays with her baby. Next a stranger enters the room and engages the baby, and the mother leaves the room. The mother reenters the room and is reunited with the baby and the stranger exits, leaving the mother and baby alone. Then the mother leaves the room again, leaving the baby alone, and finally she returns and is reunited a second time with the baby.

This critical research highlighted the importance of secure attachment for the well-being and mental health of babies. How a child responds in the Strange Situation and how securely attached he is at twelve months old seem to dictate his emotional health and emotional competence as an adult.

Ainsworth found that *securely attached* babies were upset when their mothers left the room but sought physical closeness, were easily comforted, and overall seemed happy to see their mother on her return. Between eight and eighteen months old, secure babies cycled between attachment and exploration: exploring the world using their body and newly found motor skills, and returning to the physical proximity of their mother, whom they used as a secure base from which to begin exploring again.

She found that babies who were *insecurely attached* to their mothers fell into one of two categories: They either had a consistent strategy to deal with their mother's attachment difficulties, as in the case of *insecure avoidant* babies or *insecure ambivalent* babies, or they had no clear strategy, like *insecure disorganized* babies. Ainsworth, and later Beebe, found it was overall better for the baby's mental health to be avoidant or ambivalent than disorganized.

Babies who seemed uninterested or did not respond to their mother's departure with much emotion were classified as *insecure avoidant*. They did not seek much contact with their mothers before the separation and seemed to be able to occupy themselves with toys and objects in the room. They seemed interested in the stranger and could allow her to calm them when their mother left the room; they reacted only when they were left completely alone. These babies relied on their own resources to self-regulate rather than relying on their mother as a source of comfort.

Insecure avoidant babies adapt to their absent mothers by detaching emotionally and avoiding the pain of a relationship with their mother. Insecure avoidant children often lack empathy and show signs of uncontrolled aggression and anger at a young age; these children often come to the attention of parent guidance experts, therapists, and teachers when they go to preschool. They may be the bullies of the class or seek negative attention when they are in distress or hurt; they tend to withdraw rather than seek comfort from their mother. They may express their distress and anxiety physically, which is why many are mislabeled as having ADHD.

Insecure ambivalent babies were emotionally volatile, and clingy when their mother left and hysterical when she returned. They suffered from intense separation anxiety and were unable to be easily comforted by their mother and were often angry at her. Their mothers were often anxious, and these babies absorbed their mothers' fear and anxiety and rarely felt safe in the world or trusted those around them to comfort them. They clung to their mothers and rarely learned to regulate their own emotions.

Insecure disorganized babies alternated between different methods of coping: one moment ignoring their mother and pushing her away, and the next moment clinging desperately. They were often very angry at the mother and unable to be comforted easily. Though their first impulse may be to seek comfort, when these babies are close to their mother, they feel frightened of precisely the person who should be comforting them with their fears. In the Strange Situation conditions, these babies may run up to their mother when she returns to the room, then pull away and curl up in a ball. Or they may become very aggressive and hit or throw things at the parent. They may alternate between crying and laughing.

Attachment security is passed down generationally from mother to child. In all of these cases of attachment disorders, the mother is absent in one way or another. Psychoanalyst and clinical psychologist Peter Fonagy proposed that the defensive strategy most available to the child is the one that their attachment figure—most often their mother—habitually uses in response to distress, which they then make their own.[43]

The Adult Attachment Interview (AAI) was developed by Mary Main and colleagues, inspired by Mary Ainsworth, in 1984 to explore how our early attachment relationships impact our emotional health in adulthood and how early attachment relationships impact and correlate with parenting styles. Main wanted to discover what kinds of mothers were related to these attachment difficulties and whether these strategies were passed down to the next generation.[44] She discovered the following.

Secure mothers create secure babies who grow up to be secure mothers. Secure mothers are emotionally present without being intrusive and use nonverbal communication, such as eye contact, facial expression, tone of voice, posture, and gestures, matching the infant's emotional state. The secure mother allows the baby to be upset or angry without taking it personally or feeling rejected and waits patiently for the baby to turn again toward her to engage. She addresses her baby's feelings but allows a few moments to let the baby try to resolve some of his feelings without rushing in. The secure mother transforms the baby's feelings of anger into love by responding to her baby in an empathic manner: When the baby cries and seems to reject her, the secure mother does not automatically feel rejected or hurt. She remains calm, accepts the baby's strong emotions, and soothes the baby with her body and her words. Her ability to think about what the baby is feeling and to feel what the baby is feeling helps her through this trying moment.

Dismissive mothers often create insecure avoidant babies who grow up to become dismissive mothers. In her paper "The Renunciation of Love: Dismissive Attachment and Its Treatment," Dr. Mary Connors describes dismissive attachment accurately and poetically using a line from T. S. Eliot, describing those with the condition as "renouncing love . . . a world in which desire, striving and wishes for love are repudiated."[45] A baby with a dismissive mother may turn away from love entirely to protect herself from the danger and pain of rejection.

Dismissive mothers often misread their baby's emotional cues or misunderstand the feelings the baby displays. These mothers struggle to comfort their babies when they are in distress and are more comfortable when their babies are in a good mood or are playful. These mothers often misread their baby's negative emotions, particularly when those emotions are directed toward them. They are much less likely to ask their children about their angry feelings than are mothers of securely attached children.

Dismissive mothers tend to make work or other activities a priority over relationships or love. I often hear these mothers describe the dependency of their children as uncomfortable; they avoid dependency and intimacy out of a deep-seated fear of rejection. They may be prone to postpartum depression, anxiety disorders, and sleep disorders; they may turn to alcohol or food to escape and to reduce tension. One of my patients said to me, "I was supposed to take a three-month maternity leave. But when my boss called and asked if I could come back to the office at eight weeks, I couldn't wait to leave." Some mommy blogs have given women a forum to vent this kind of anger and resentment at having to meet their child's needs; by saying publicly what they (and many other women) have felt privately, they want to normalize those feelings. For many women who read those blogs and essays, it's a relief to find that they're not the only ones who aren't comfortable with nurturing. But while these fears of dependency and intimacy may be common, they're not healthy.

Angie came to see me because her three-year-old daughter, Lauren, had been throwing tantrums. Lauren had started to hit other children and became aggressive with the teachers when they asked her to follow the rules of the classroom. Angie felt Lauren was angry at her, but didn't understand why. Lauren had a caregiver she liked, and Angie made it a point to be home in time to put Lauren to bed almost every night. Angie was exhausted when she returned from work each night and had little energy for her daughter's needs and demands. Angie was a believer that children should be independent as soon as possible; that was how she was raised. Working with me, Angie realized her own mother had found her needy and demanding. When she was able to experience the pain of her mother's rejection, Angie was able to be more patient and empathetic with her daughter, who responded by becoming calmer and less angry.

Preoccupied, anxious mothers often create insecure ambivalent babies who grow up to become preoccupied, anxious mothers. A preoccupied, anxious mother is emotionally unavailable even when she is physically present. These mothers tend to be emotionally intense and fragile and often use their babies to help reassure them or regulate their emotions, rather than doing so for their children. They worry incessantly and carry fears of abandonment and loss from their own childhood and have a hard time with separation in all of their relationships. They can be intrusive, like a helicopter mother, and inconsistent with their attention: engaged with their child when he is happy, but turning away if he is in distress. These mothers often have a difficult time reading their baby's emotional cues because they are so preoccupied with their own fears and worries.

Disorganized mothers often create insecure disorganized babies who grow up to become disorganized mothers. A disorganized mother is the most unpredictable mother in terms of her behavior and can go between extreme depression and extreme anger. She has difficulty in regulating her own behavior and emotions, and her rage leads her to shame her child. She lacks both self-regulation and regulation by others, and when she is stressed becomes scary and induces fear in her child.

A baby's attachment experiences—good and bad—are based on repeated experiences and continuous interactions with her mother. When a mother is not present physically and emotionally, these interactions are interrupted. It is her mother who helps a child to develop a sense of herself in the world by acknowledging her as an individual. Psychoanalysts like Peter Fonagy, György Gergely, and Mary Target believe that when a baby sees herself through her mother's eyes, it is the foundation of a secure sense of self. When she is in distress or frightened as she grows up, it is her mother's comforting voice inside her head that reassures her. These early experiences of a baby being understood on an emotional level by her mother develop what Schore calls the "implicit self"[46] or Winnicott calls the "true self."[47]

Bowlby's theory that the brain constructs working models of the self, attachment figures, and the environment[48] can be validated by neuroimaging of the human brain. We now know that a baby's brain contains mirror neurons from birth; these allow the baby to simulate or mimic the facial expressions and gestures of his mother. The development of these neurons is encouraged by a mother's responses, which show a baby that he has been understood. It is through this process of mothers and babies interacting and sharing emotions, expressions, and gestures that a baby develops an understanding of his own, and others', emotions and intentions.

It is clear that healthy and secure attachment is the first step in a long emotional journey necessary for emotional regulation, resilience to stress, good self-esteem, and the ability to have healthy relationships in the future. The time and effort we put into our children in the first three years to ensure this healthy attachment is worth all the sacrifice we may have to make.

CHAPTER 4

Presence 101

Being Present and Engaged to Meet Your Baby's Needs

Patients often ask me for concrete advice on how to change their child's behavior. My answer is always the same: The best way I can help a child is to help his parents be more self-aware of their own feelings and behaviors and how they impact their child. If you are reading this book, chances are you are already focused on being the best, most present mother you can be. Presence requires focus and a set of skills that come fairly naturally to some and takes more work for others, but I believe it can be taught to every woman. One of the essential characteristics of a present mother is her ability to be comfortable *in the present* or in the moment; this state is sometimes referred to as mindfulness. Dr. Joe Loizzo, founder of the Nalanda Institute and a psychotherapist who specializes in integrating Buddhist teaching into clinical work, told me that being mindful means "that our self-awareness is engaged . . . and you are actually able to observe what's happening. This is a key element of parenting."[1]

The ability to be in the moment and feel that there is no place you would rather be, no one else you would rather be with, and nothing else you would rather be doing is a powerful thing. In his book *Journey of Awakening*, Ram Dass talked about the three pillars of life: the doing, the having, and the being.[2] Being is the most important pillar for a healthy self, healthy relationships, and a purposeful life, but most people work their whole lives *doing* so that they can *have* more, and spend little if any time *being*. If we cannot be quiet and at peace with ourselves, then it is much harder to be with our babies (or in any deep and meaningful relationship).

It is essential that to be fully engaged in the present, we have made peace with the past. Busyness and activity can suppress the memories and feelings of traumatic events or painful relationships; when we are quiet or unoccupied, we often are flooded with these painful memories and feelings. A mother who has unresolved conflicts and painful feelings about her own mother may be able to sit on the floor with her baby for a little while but soon may feel sad, bored, or even sleepy and want to get away from the quiet and away from her baby.

In this chapter you'll find *practical* ways of being present and engaging with your baby. You will find many of these suggestions are easy to implement, although others may be more difficult. While it's important to make these methods part of your routine with your baby, it's also important to explore and reflect on your feelings if any of these techniques feel uncomfortable or don't seem to work for you.

Presence Means Removing Distraction

We are a society of multitaskers—checking email while eating dinner, searching the Web while we channel surf, texting a friend while we have a conversation with another friend. Research has shown that this constant distraction and dividing of our attention affects our ability to hold focus on one activity or relationship for a long period of time. Women in general and mothers in particular are called on to share not only their attention but also their emotional and physical energy, and there is a limit to what we can share. It is harmful to our relationships with our children when we try to interact with them while doing multiple other things. Eye contact and nonverbal cues are a very important part of your emotional presence. You may believe you are present with your child, but if your mind and attention are not on your child, you are *not* in fact emotionally present. If you are doing the dishes and talking to your child, or cleaning while talking to your child, you are not being present, you're distracted.

> If your mind and attention are not on your child, you are *not* in fact emotionally present.

It is rare for me to walk down the street or go for a walk in the park and to see a mother or caregiver truly engaged with a baby. Instead, I see mothers and caregivers preoccupied with their cell phones. Technology has changed our lives forever, in some ways for the good and in some ways not. The desire to be stimulated every moment and to flee from the boring moments of being with our babies is only exacerbated by the seduction of our constantly lit-up cell phones. One might say (and I do) that we did better before the ubiquitous cell phone in terms of our focus on our children. As a culture we have become inured to the impact of these interruptions and distractions on our feelings, our psyches, and our sense of self. My husband and I recently went to a restaurant and had dinner near a couple who looked at their cell phones, not each other, for the entire dinner. Imagine what it is like for your child when you constantly pick up your phone, text, or check your emails to see if there is something or someone more important and more interesting than he is. It is your ability to find your child interesting that makes your child feel interesting and develops his self-esteem; of course, constantly checking your phone will make your child feel less interesting and less important to you.

So what can you do to ensure that you are plugged in to your baby and not technology?

- Mute your phone when you are walking down the street with your baby. Before the age of six months, your baby should be facing you in the stroller, so that you can make eye contact and engage her as much as possible.

- Inform your nanny or caregiver that there will be a strict no phone policy while he or she is on duty. The caregiver should use a cell phone only in an emergency or to reach you.

- Make sure your baby can see you when you speak to her. Don't talk to her from another room.

- Turn off the TV and radio when you are not actively listening to them or when you notice your child is not listening to them.

- If you work outside the home or are away for most of the day, place a basket near the front door and place your phone in it. When you come home, mute your phone and/or tablet. You can turn your device(s) on after your child is asleep or goes down for a nap. If you must be available and keep your phone with you (if you are a doctor on call, for example), set your phone or pager on vibrate.

- Inform your work, friends, and family that you will be not be responding to calls, texts, or emails for specific periods of time unless it is a true emergency.

If unplugging yourself from your devices is difficult or uncomfortable for you, ask yourself why. Is the droning of superficial information and constant contact with others drowning out feelings of dissatisfaction, boredom, sadness, or anger? And consider this study from the University of Indiana, which found that children have shorter attention spans when their parents are distracted by cell phones and other technology.[3]

If you're having trouble transitioning from work or outside activities to being present with your child, you may find that yoga can help. A study from the University of Manchester in England showed that yoga lowered mothers' cortisol levels so they were calmer, less anxious, and more available to their infants.[4] Meditative yoga is often associated with mindfulness or the ability to be emotionally present without distractions in a world full of distractions; it has been shown to be very helpful to mothers who suffer from anxiety, but has limits in terms of helping mothers with even mild depression unless the practice involves, as Randi Coen-Gilbert, a Philadelphia-based birth doula and mother–infant yoga teacher, said to me, "Eyes wide open and contact with others. Isolation is not what a mother who already feels isolated needs more of; rather, she needs to feel connected to those around her while feeling connected to herself and to her baby."

The practice of mindfulness is the moment-to-moment, nonjudgmental awareness of our experience; by identifying and naming emotions and sensations, we can lessen feelings of anxiety, agitation, and boredom. Mindfulness can promote deep relaxation, which leads to feeling less stress and an increased resilience to its effects. For example, when we are aware of the places we feel achy or stiff or where we just plain hurt, we can respond to the physical pain as individual experiences rather than identifying with the pain as if it were all there is. The same goes for emotional experiences.

_____

All mothers can benefit from the practice of mindfulness.

_____

All mothers can benefit from the practice of mindfulness. You'll find some simple exercises, some for you and some for you and your child, created by mindfulness teacher Nancy Fischer Mortifee, in Appendix B.

Presence Means Recognizing the Importance of Empathy and Attunement

Empathy is the ability to feel or intuit another living creature's feelings or to be able to put ourselves in another person's shoes emotionally. Empathy is not something we are born with; it is something we learn from the earliest relationship with our mother or primary caregiver. If our mother is empathic or has the capacity to feel for us, then we learn to feel for others. Our first experience of feeling that we exist is in the reflection of our emotions in our mother's face, and later through her words. We learn and internalize empathy when our mother is attuned to our feelings, meaning she can read our nonverbal cues and intuit our emotions and our needs through our facial expression, body language, cries and sounds, and eye contact (or lack thereof) and show us she understands how we feel by what psychoanalysts and attachment researchers call mirroring or primary reflection. This ability to read a baby's cues comes from the mother's right side of the brain; at the moment of attunement, the mother's right brain is communicating with the baby's right brain. For example, if a baby has downturned lips, tears in her eyes, a red face, and is beginning to cry, her mother responds by making a sad face herself and speaks softly and comforts her baby; this shows the baby her feelings are recognized, understood, validated, and accepted by her mother. This interaction is the beginning of the baby's development of a sense of herself as a valuable and loved person and is the start of learning empathic responses.

When a mother's response does not reflect her baby's emotions but either dismisses or tries to override them, a baby becomes confused and frightened—for example, a mother meets her baby's sad face with a bored, disinterested, or angry expression, looks away, or responds with a great big smile and loud, cheerful voice. To the baby, such a response says his mother does not understand his feelings or that what he is feeling doesn't matter, and therefore *he* doesn't matter. A baby develops ways to cope with misattunement: He may turn from his mother, cry and cling to her, or alternate between the two. As I said earlier, if a mother is physically present but emotionally unable to connect with her child, it can be as painful for her child as if she were not there at all.

One surprisingly simple way to connect to your baby and make him feel more secure is to cradle him on your left side, rather than your right. Not only is the reassuring beat of your heart more audible, but the line of vision between the two of you enhances right brain to right brain communication. If you're breastfeeding, start your baby on the right side and finish on the left; if you're bottle-feeding, snuggle your baby on your left side. If your baby is upset, you may find that cradling him on your left side while you comfort him calms him more quickly.[5]

Temporary misinterpretations or missteps are part of the moment-to-moment relationship between mother and child; *all* mothers experience it. It is *how aware* you are of these missteps and how quickly you can repair the lapse in communication by acknowledging the baby's feelings and soothing her distress that matters. (I'll talk more about this in Chapter 8.)

However, if emotional misattunement becomes chronic, it can lead to a child having an impaired ability to be empathic or to read others' emotional cues. When a toddler consistently pushes, touches, or hits another child to get his attention even though that child is clearly indicating that he is angry, frustrated, or bothered, she is showing that she has difficulty reading emotional cues. A child who lacks empathy will not care if the friend she pushed on the playground is hurt or if a friend is upset after her block tower is knocked down. This does not mean an occasional lapse in the ability to care about another child's feelings, but a pattern of behavior. All children have bad days, but it is the consistency of the behavior that should grab your attention.

Presence Means Regulating Your Child's Emotions

Babies are born with an underdeveloped central nervous system and have no way of negotiating internal and external sensations and experiences without the help of their mother or primary caregiver. According to researcher Nim Tottenham, primary caregivers (and, most important, mothers, I believe) act as an extension of that nervous system until children are about two years old.[6]

Emotional regulation requires both interest in and focus on your baby. This is easier said than done if you are anxious or easily bored and distracted when you are with your child or you don't find your own child interesting because you don't allow yourself to become engaged with her. I always say to my patients that if you don't find your baby fascinating to be with then why should anyone else—a caregiver, for instance—find her fascinating?

It's hard being a baby! Your infant lives in a scary, confusing, complicated, and demanding world. You help your child interpret and regulate his emotions and keep him in a balanced state, both physically and emotionally; this is called emotional homeostasis. The ability to regulate our emotions means we can be angry without losing our temper, can experience sadness without getting depressed, and can be happy without becoming manic. Resilience is the ability to return to a regulated emotional state after being excited or upset. While it's critical for our emotional health that we can rely on others to comfort us in times of difficulty, it's equally important to be able to regulate our own emotions. The secure child, and later the secure adult, is one who can shift easily between self-soothing and asking others for support when he is under stress.

Emotional regulation is a two-step process: nonverbal, or primary, regulation and then verbal, or secondary, regulation. It is a dance between a mother and a baby. This dance requires that you are attuned to your baby's feelings as well as to your own. This means being aware of your own feelings, both conscious and unconscious at that moment, which will be communicated to your baby through your voice, your facial expressions, and through your body language and which impact your baby's developing emotional world.

The primary emotions—sadness, joy, anger, surprise, fear, disgust, and shame—are universal across cultures and displayed through facial expressions and bodily nonverbal cues. Emotions are somatic, or felt in our bodies, and emotional regulation is a bodily process. When we are in a hyperaroused state our heart races, and when we are hypoaroused it slows down. When you regulate your baby's emotions, you are either downregulating or calming (bringing your baby gently down from a heightened state of joy, surprise, fear, and anger), or upregulating or exciting (gently bringing your baby up from a state of sadness, disgust, or shame).

The first step in emotional regulation is nonverbal or primary regulation, an unconscious process in which you use your right brain to read your baby's body-based emotional cues—through eye contact, touch, posture, vocal sounds and rhythms, and facial expression—and then mirror her expressions.

Eye contact is the most intense form of nonverbal communication between a mother and a baby; it excites, soothes, and resonates with a baby's physical and emotional state, linking her nervous system with that of her mother. If a baby has a mother who is nonresponsive or does not make enough eye contact, she learns to disengage physically and emotionally from the relationship, which becomes a kind of learned helplessness. In a healthy mother–baby relationship, a baby will avert her eyes when she is overstimulated or has had enough play; this is natural. Let her take a moment and don't feel rejected when she turns away or keep trying to get her attention. She'll let you know when she wants you again, soon enough!

Your facial expressions, body posture, and even gestures provide important emotional cues for your baby. Your face clearly expresses empathy versus disinterest, patience versus anger, calm versus anxiety. When you and your baby are on the same level, you indicate your interest and attention, as you do when you lean in toward the baby. Frantic or anxious waving or movement can overwhelm or frighten your child, so stay present but don't overexaggerate.

Researcher Judi Mesman observed that American mothers often tend to entertain their babies in a way mothers in the rest of the world do less often. Although Mesman has not yet compared these cultural patterns statistically, her observations of hundreds of mothers and babies from different cultures lead her to hypothesize that this overly exuberant, overstimulating, over-the-top positive show of emotion to elicit a smile or laugh in a baby seems "to come from some need in the mothers to be reassured that their babies like them or love them. If they don't get a smile or laugh they feel rejected or insecure." Mesman noted that some American mothers' faces would fall if their baby didn't respond with positive emotion when they interacted with them or they would say, "Don't you like Mommy anymore?" Mesman's impression is that in other countries, mothers were more likely to allow their baby to be in whatever mood he was in at the time and spent much less time in stimulating play and attempts to make the baby smile. Of course, the mothers played with their babies and smiled and made silly faces at them when it was clear the baby was interested and engaged, but instead of putting energy and effort into cajoling the baby to smile, mothers instead tended to reflect whatever feelings the babies had at the moment. These interactions had a quieter feel to them, more like taking a walk in the park rather than going to the circus.[7]

Verbal or secondary emotional regulation builds on successful nonverbal emotional regulation. It is a conscious, left-brain-centered process in which you use your imagination to interpret what your baby is feeling based on her nonverbal cues and put those feelings into words. So when you recognize that your baby is sad (right brain), you mirror her sad face with your own, then say to your baby (left brain), "You seem sad." You might go further by not only thinking about *what* your baby may be feeling but also *why*: "I wonder if you are feeling sad because Mommy left the room for a moment?" This is the process of verbal reflection, where the right brain (emotional development) and the left brain (cognitive development) meet and work together.

Of course, you're not always going to get it right; communication between mothers and babies is an art more than a science, and you must be present to learn to interpret what your baby is telling you. It's like learning a language; you have to put in the hours if you want to be fluent. If you say to your baby, "You sound hungry," and she is not hungry, when you try to feed her she will let you know you were wrong. You will try again until you get it right and then tell

> Communication between mothers and babies is an art more than a science.

your baby, "Mommy is so sorry she got it wrong; you wanted Mommy to pick you up." If your child is difficult to comfort and soothe, remember that she may be cold or hungry, wet or tired; her stomach may hurt, or her head may be throbbing; she may be scared you will leave or may have had a bad dream. A pediatrician once suggested to me that if you're unsure what your preverbal baby wants, first assume hunger, then a wet or full diaper, other physical discomfort (too hot, too cold, uncomfortable clothing), and finally emotional distress (which includes overstimulation).

Many mothers are afraid to try to interpret their baby's feelings for fear they will make a mistake. But babies are very forgiving when their mothers make mistakes, as long as they keep trying to understand what their babies need. It is when mothers stop trying or don't even bother to try that babies feel abandoned, as if they lived in a world where they speak Greek but no one else does or, worse, that they are being ignored altogether. If you are unavailable, emotionally or physically, to your child when she is in distress, then she is quite literally alone with her pain.

When your child is a toddler, he will be in constant conflict over internalizing the rules and structure expected of him by society—which is often the opposite of his desires. By the time he can speak, he will be confronted with a set of emotional challenges and conflicts that is so upsetting that most adults have repressed their memories of the pain of that time and cannot remember those events years later. I tell the parents who come to me that what a toddler is going through is like swallowing an elephant. Even a big glass of chocolate milk doesn't help it to go down.

Having a toddler is challenging for parents too. Toddlers are often frustrated, angry, out of control, or fighting for control, often at the same time (perfectly normal for a toddler). Around the age of three you can expect some aggressive behavior—often toward a mother by her daughter and a father by his son—as your child goes through what psychoanalysts call Oedipal development, when a child becomes deeply attached to the parent of the opposite sex and sees the same-sex parent as unwelcome competition. This usually resolves around the age of six. Yet knowing all of this is useless unless you can empathize with your child about how hard it is to grow up.

Trying to discipline a child before she develops a conscience (that internal voice that tells her she's doing something wrong, an important developmental milestone) and is able to internalize a sense of rules and structure is pretty much useless; for most children, this happens around twenty-four months. The best way to help a child to control her behavior when she is a toddler is to help her name and understand her emotions when she is a baby. However, I'm sorry to have to tell you, teaching your toddler to regulate her emotions does not help you escape tantrums, which are like blown emotional fuses.

A toddler feels pulled between her own desires and the expectations of her parents; the struggle is both physically and emotionally painful for her. When you put your child's feelings into words, it not only makes her feel understood but also helps her gain control over and contain her impulses and increases her tolerance for frustration. For instance, you pass a toy store and your child demands that you go in and buy her a toy. Rather than simply saying, "You can't have a toy," try saying, "I hear that you are upset and angry because you want a toy and Mommy is saying no. I know it's hard to hear the word *no* and not get everything you want when you want it." Or when your child has a tantrum because she wants to go to the park after school and you have to take her to a doctor's appointment, rather than saying, "No, we can't go to the park today," say something like, "I can see you want to go to the park because being at school all day was hard and you want to play. I know you feel sad and angry because you want to play and we have to go to the doctor instead." It also helps to touch or offer physical affection to a child who is feeling out of control, if she will accept it. What is most important is that you do not leave her presence while she is upset. The ability to remain calm and in control of your feelings is key when helping your toddler learn to regulate her own feelings and eventually learn to calm herself. In psychoanalytic terms, your infant is all id, an unconscious jumble of desires and emotions, and you are her external conscience (like Jiminy Cricket, aka the superego), setting boundaries and rules of behavior. Eventually, your child will internalize your voice and rules and be able to negotiate between her desires and appropriate and socially acceptable behavior.

Presence Means Maternal Self-Awareness

Are you aware of when you are feeling angry, frustrated, shut down, bored, or anxious or when you are putting on a happy face to cover your real feelings? Are you in touch with *why* you're feeling the way you do? It is this self-knowledge that is at the core of mindfulness and presence, and it is your patience, affection, calm, and containment that help your baby weather emotional storms.

The ability to soothe and comfort your baby when he is distressed is possible only if you are in control of your own emotions and aware of how your baby's distress makes *you* feel. One of the most important things you can do as a mother is to recognize and acknowledge your baby's feelings of distress or pain and be with him when he is distressed rather than distracting or cheering him up or, even worse, dismissing his feelings because he makes you uncomfortable.

Many mothers feel rejected by their babies when they cannot comfort them easily and turn away from their babies' distress response. If you have difficulty being present with your child when he is upset, you may have unresolved conflicts or issues from your own childhood. When a mother has to work or take time for herself, some feelings of guilt are natural. Some mothers have a very intense stress response when confronted with their babies' distress. In fact, mothers who suffer from postpartum depression have very high cortisol levels in response to their baby's cries, which is like a PTSD response.[8] Yoga and meditation can help calm these reactions, and counseling or psychotherapy can help. In the beginning, we know ourselves by looking at the empathic face of our mothers, but if we did not see what we needed to see in our mother's face and eyes, we can seek that empathic look in the eyes and face of a therapist. This is the beginning of healing and of being able to reflect our own baby's emotions.

Presence Means Recognizing and Accepting Guilty Feelings

Guilt is a signal feeling that tells us we are in conflict. It alerts us that we have unfinished emotional business or that we are ambivalent about a decision. When a mother has to work or take time for herself, some feelings of guilt are natural, and expected.

Guilt is a very difficult feeling for mothers to handle, and ignoring or repressing those feelings often results in a mother turning away from her baby. When a mother tells me she feels guilty, I encourage her to look at and recognize her conflicts, not to turn away from those feelings. When we ignore the signs of conflict or ambivalence and consciously push them away, we ignore our *selves*. This denial tends to cause more problems for us and our relationships in the long run. However, when we confront our conflicts and turn *toward* our guilty feelings, we have a greater chance of resolving them in a satisfying way. If a mother feels guilty leaving her very young baby, and society, her partner, and her work tell her, "Don't worry, don't feel guilty it's okay," they are denying a simple truth—it may *not* be okay for *that* mother or *that* baby.

Some guilt is excessive and disruptive to the relationship between a mother and baby—that's called anxiety—but for the most part, guilt is a message sent by our unconscious that we may not be striking the right balance in our lives.

Presence Means Allowing Your Baby to Feel Some Frustration

To become a healthy adult, everyone needs to be able to tolerate some frustration. When it comes to babies and toddlers, however, there is a lot of confusion about what amount of "some frustration" is appropriate. Babies experience some small frustration when their mothers cannot feed them quickly enough or cannot change their diaper immediately. As Mesman said, even babies whose mothers "wear" them, or carry them constantly, cry sometimes (they just cry less). A present mother does not ignore the cries of her child but allows a little time for her baby to show discomfort, gradually increasing the amount of time before she responds with her voice and touch. However, she responds before her baby becomes overwhelmed by his feelings or over-stressed.

This delayed response allows the baby to begin to try to self-soothe, but it does not mean letting a young baby "cry it out." When a baby under the age of one cries, he needs you to soothe him. The most disturbing thing for me to see when I am in public is a baby whose parents or caregivers allow him to cry to the point of hysteria. When I intervene (which I do often) I am usually told, "It's just that he is tired and is trying to sleep." So let me set the record straight: If a baby is crying, he needs you. Period. Even when your baby is trying to fall asleep, he is facing his fear of the dark, fear of aloneness, fear of separation, and fear of his own aggression and yours. So letting your baby cry, as in Ferber's recommendations for sleep training, just confirms that the world is a scary and untrustworthy place where your child's emotional needs will not get met and may foster the kind of defensive behavior I see later in many of my patients.

Before the age of one, your baby's cries should always be assumed to be caused by need or fear, but after the age of one, children may cry for many reasons, including frustration and anger. How you soothe your child does not change. If your child is angry or frustrated, it is important that you remain calm in the face of his anger and, as with a younger child, use empathy and understanding. You might use a reflective statement, which helps put your child's feelings into words, such as, "You sound mad at Mommy right now, and it's okay, Mommy is here, and it's okay to be angry at me." Or, "You seem upset at Mommy because I didn't pick you up right away. It's okay to be upset, and Mommy is here now."

Presence Means Talking to Your Child

Studies have shown that mothers who talk to their babies, not only expressing their own emotions but also accurately putting their baby's feelings into words, raise children who can, in turn, easily express their emotions and are less prone to depression and anxiety.[9]

The more you talk to your baby about your feelings and comment on her feelings and your shared experiences, the more you help her understand both her internal and her external world. When you point out a bird sitting on a branch and say, "Look! There is a beautiful bird, and it is singing such a sweet song. How happy that makes me!," you are teaching your baby not just to observe but to describe her experiences and feelings. Given the similarities between the toddler and adolescent brain, doing this now will help your child (and you!) when she is a tween and teenager.

Mothers often ask me, "Why talk to my baby when he can't understand me?" or tell me, "My husband and I fight in front of our baby because he can't understand anyway." While babies and toddlers may not have a lot of spoken language, they do understand body language and facial expressions and what your tone of voice conveys. And they learn pretty quickly to connect your words to what you're really feeling and your nonverbal cues.

Presence Means Playing with Your Child

The right brain is the seat of creativity, playfulness, humor, and spontaneity.[10] When you play with your baby, you stimulate her right brain as well as your own.

> When you play with your baby, you stimulate her right brain as well as your own.

Play is one of the most important parts of being a child; it is the language of children. Children must learn to play before they learn their letters and numbers; a child who has not learned to play will have problems emotionally, socially, and academically. Play is how children develop their imagination, how they master their environment, how they communicate, and how they work through conflicts and gain a sense of control and power. Play is a way of sharing their inner world with you. It is their occupation and their delight, and their way both of being social and of retreating from social interaction. It is how children safely explore their feelings, develop their self-esteem, work on their physical and social skills, and learn to cope with frustration.

Playing with your baby is a powerful form of interaction. We know that when a mother plays with her baby it fosters the development of the social emotional parts of the brain and helps regulate his emotions. Play is a way for mothers and babies to bond in the excitement of a shared moment. When you sit and interact with your baby but also allow him to play independently of you, it promotes the beginning of healthy separation, autonomy, and healthy interdependence.

Getting down on the floor with your child will bring out your most playful self. Playtime will happen on your child's schedule, not yours. This is a time to give your child your full attention. Let her decide what she wants to do and follow her lead. You can model playing with toys or blocks or demonstrate how a toy works, but let your child make mistakes and resist the urge to show her the "correct" way to finger paint or arrange her pile of blocks. You can narrate her activity ("You're picking up the blue block") and participate in the play ("Would you like a green block too?"). Be sensitive to how much stimulation your child can handle, look at her body language to see whether the music is too loud or too many toys are overwhelming her. Let her express *all* her feelings, even if they make you uncomfortable. If your child seems to lose interest in a toy, you can offer her another, but don't get upset if she no longer wants to play with you.

Birth to Twelve Months: Mommy, Entertain Me, and I Will Entertain You

In the first year, your baby is exploring his world, especially with his mouth. Age-appropriate toys like rattles, mobiles, chew toys, and soft cloth books are stimulating but not frustrating. This is the time to hand toys to your baby or place toys within his reach and allow him to explore while you watch.

Whether you and your baby are swaying to Bach or dancing to your favorite rock band, music stimulates the right brain. And don't be shy about singing: All babies love their mommy's voice, no matter how they sound.

Be sensitive to your baby's nonverbal communication and the very special dance between you and your baby. If he is overstimulated and turns away, wait quietly until he turns his face back to you. You can help your baby feel powerful and confident in his abilities by encouraging him to reach for and grasp objects or your hand. Encourage your baby to shake his rattle rather than shaking it for him. Games like rolling a ball back and forth between you and your baby gives him a sense of control.

Playing peekaboo helps your baby practice separating. Hiding objects and making them reappear helps your baby learn object constancy, the understanding that even when they can't see something, it still exists. This translates into the capacity to understand that when you go away you will return.

Twelve to Twenty-four Months: Little Explorers

Toddlers love to be physical; jumping, climbing, and running help them feel competent and develop their motor skills. They are also fascinated by their poop. It's a normal part of development. Offer your child Play-Doh and finger paints.

Toddlers love manipulative toys such as blocks, which help them feel mastery over objects. Push and pull toys demonstrate cause and effect; the fun is in the process rather than the end product. Shape sorters, nesting cups, and simple puzzles help children develop problem-solving skills.

Your toddler loves to be read to and will often memorize the books you read to her—over and over. The repetition, though it may be frustrating for you, is comforting for your child.

At this age, children are most interested in playing with their mother or primary caregiver and will play side by side with other children their age rather than interact. This is called *parallel play*, and if you've seen two adults sitting together, each absorbed in his own cell phone, you've seen parallel play. The point is, parallel play is a normal developmental stage for children, which they outgrow when they learn to interact with one another in a two-way relationship. (Unless they don't, which leads to social difficulty in adulthood.)

Imaginary play allows toddlers to work through emotional conflicts and fears; watching and playing with your toddler will teach you a great deal about your child's unconscious feelings, fears, and wishes. Pay attention to what your child needs from you: If she wants you to watch her play, then watch, if she wants you to be the evil queen be the evil queen.

Twenty-four to Thirty-six Months: Join Me in My Pretend World

After two years old, playdates become part of the family calendar. Children play together and are more eager for playmates other than their mother, though they may revert to parallel play when they're tired.

Children of this age can internalize structure and rules, and, as a result of their increased language, physical competence, and problem-solving skills, they are more prepared to be part of group situations, like preschool. This is the time when children are also learning to resolve conflicts and tolerate more frustration, as they have to share toys and take turns.

On the other hand, this is a very aggressive age where children are testing their (and your) limits and often resisting the rules. As they struggle with their sexual development (yes, it really does begin this early), which involves choosing one parent over another as their romantic love object, children often develop (and express) more fears—of the dark, monsters, and loud noises—as they learn to deal with their own aggressive and guilty feelings. Remember, when a child wants to possess one parent exclusively (as a little girl who wants to marry her daddy), she must reject the other, and this can cause guilty feelings, which are difficult for any child to process.

Fantasy play continues to be important as their imagination grows. Simple props and dress-up clothes will keep them occupied for quite a while. They will want you to join them; do. Children will use toy animals, dollhouses, and dolls to act out stories and express their feelings. You can learn a great deal just by observing and listening as they do.

With potty training on the horizon, tactile materials like sand, mud, Play-Doh, clay, and finger paints offer more socially and hygienically acceptable ways of playing with their poop.

Simple board games help your child understand rules and develop concepts of fairness and right and wrong. Your child may become more competitive in games and insist on winning. It's okay once in a while to let her win, even if she hasn't actually won; it helps her develop a sense of competence.

Presence Means Helping Ease Transitions and Separations

As children begin to explore the world, they practice separation. As they become mobile, they use their mothers as what psychoanalysts Margaret Mahler, Fred Pine, and Annie Bergman called "emotional refueling stations."[11] First this means staying very close to their mother, like an ice skater holding on to the railing of the ice rink. Later they use her as a safe base from which to explore, always returning to touch her or make eye contact (which is like, as Mahler and other researchers have said, touch from a distance),[12] however briefly, to make sure she is still there. Secure attachment makes separation less painful for children, but separation causes a child pain even when that child has an emotionally present mother.

From the age of three months on, a child realizes his mother is his environment and can satisfy or deprive him of what he needs. At six to eight months, he becomes aware that his mother can leave and not return, and what we call separation anxiety begins in earnest. From then until eighteen to twenty-two months, children feel bound to their mothers as the source of their security, and when she is not present either physically or emotionally, they develop fearful feelings.

The most painful times for young children are the comings and goings of their mothers. Babies need security, consistency, and predictability from their mothers, especially during times of transition, such as waking up, going down for and waking up from a nap; moving to and from daycare or preschool; and switching from playtime to bath time, from bath time to dinnertime, and from dinnertime to bedtime. When you leave the house, whether it is to go to work or to go to the supermarket or gym, it is a separation, which deserves the same respect as any other transition.

Here are some things you can do to ease the transitions or comings and goings for the baby:

- Always say good-bye when you leave your child.

- When you have to leave to go out and your baby shows distress, reflect your baby's feelings of sadness and pain and put those feelings into words. Then reassure him that you will return later, that his caregiver is there to take care of him, and that you will miss him too.

- When you are leaving, allow extra time. Let your baby be sad and angry when you leave, rather than rushing away from his feelings because they are uncomfortable for you (and him).

- Create a routine for when you leave and when you are reunited. For example, before you go out the door, tell your child what he will do during the day, who will stay with him, and when you will return. Sing a "leaving song" (no matter how silly, and my children can tell you I came up with some really bad ones) or give your child something of yours to keep until you return, a long and loving hug, and the reassurance you will return. When you return, let him return the object (if he wants to) or sit on the floor immediately, and let your child come to you on his own terms. You can play the I wonder game (I wonder what David had for lunch today? I wonder what Anna did at the playground?) with a toddler. You can involve your caregiver in the ritual too.

• Tell your baby that you will return and *when* you will return. Remember that no matter how young your baby is, she understands your intent if not the meaning of your words, and at some point (much sooner than you think) she will understand your words.

• Whenever possible, once out and once in is easier on babies then in and out, in and out. If you have to leave shortly after you return from an absence, it's better to stay away for the longer period of time.

• When you return, acknowledge your baby and her feelings at the first moment of reunion. If you have to go to the bathroom or make a call or need a few moments before you greet your baby, do it outside the home so when you walk in the door your child is your sole focus.

• Do your best to be present for the big transitions, like morning waking and going to sleep.

How your child reacts to you when you return indicates how he is coping with being separated from you, and the length of the separation. Based on my clinical experience, I have found that children who are separated from their mothers for shorter periods of time and reunited with their mothers immediately have an easier time repairing the effects of the separation. A child who is separated from his mother and then has to wait to be reunited—for example, if a babysitter picks up the child from daycare and stays with him until his mother returns from work—may have more trouble adjusting. Pay close attention in these moments to notice important cues.

A healthy reunion with your baby—whether you've been gone for one hour or eight hours—would look something like this:

> You walk in the door and your baby greets you with a smile and open arms outstretched. She meets your gaze and seeks physical contact.

or

> You walk in the door and your baby is crying for you. When you hold her, she calms quickly and is happy to see you.

> If your baby feels you have been gone too long:

> You walk in and your baby is uninterested in you, preferring his surrogate caregiver. He doesn't make eye contact with you and pulls away when you hold him.

or

> Your baby is fussy when you enter and cannot easily be soothed when you hold him.

or

Your baby is very clingy and demanding and refuses to release you for even a moment, even after you've been home for some time.

It is important that you do not turn away from the signs of your baby's needs because you feel guilty; if you do, your baby may not give you many chances to repair the separation. Think of these signs as an opportunity you are being given to make things right.

The Importance of Transitional Objects

Respect your child's need for transitional objects like blankets, stuffed animals, and/or pacifiers, which represent you and the security you provide, in your absence. The ability to self-soothe is not self-evident in all babies and is more the exception than the rule; if your child naturally takes to a transitional object, it will be easier for you to leave for short periods of time. Sometimes babies use their thumbs or toes as transitional objects to soothe themselves in your absence. I say to mothers that a baby who sucks his thumb or his hand or his foot is a very resourceful baby. Dentists are always trying to scare mothers about thumb sucking, pacifier, or nipple dependency, and yet these are the babies who do the best when separating from their mothers. There are many reasons children need braces; ignore the dentists in favor of your child's emotional health.

Washing transitional objects should be done only when the ball of dust follows your baby like the *Peanuts* character Pigpen. In fact, the smellier the transitional object the better for your baby, who relies on the comfort of the smells to feel secure. A friend told me that her daughter's stuffed Minnie Mouse got so dirty and crusted with formula and mashed bananas that she felt she *had* to wash it. When she gave her daughter the clean stuffed animal, the toddler burst into tears and wouldn't accept it. My friend spent the next hour rubbing formula and mashed bananas into Minnie's ears and the beloved object was never washed again.

Any object of yours that reminds your baby of you can serve as a transitional object. When mothers have to leave for more than an hour or two, I always recommend they take their smelliest T-shirt and let the baby hold it while they are gone. A picture of you can also serve as a transitional object; you can hang it over the crib or give it to your toddler when they have to go preschool. If you can't be there at bedtime, record yourself reading a story or singing a lullaby. One patient of mine would give her baby her key chain until she returned home. The most important thing is that you do not take your child's transitional object—whatever it is—away from him until he is ready to give it up. Depending on the sensitivity of your child and how attached he is to you, this may mean well into the beginning of kindergarten. Many mothers want to control the process of separation and want their babies to separate on their terms rather than on the baby's schedule. Babies separate in their own good time and when they are ready. Forcing them to prematurely separate may have negative consequences, as explained in Chapter 7.

Caregiver consistency is critical for separation to go well. Children need predictability, which helps them understand what will happen in the future and to feel secure in the moment. When we look at the developing world model, like Mary Ainsworth did in Uganda,[13] or at countries in which

> Babies separate in their own good time and when they are ready.

Judi Mesman did in her research,[14] we see that even where mothers rely on others to care for their children, those caregivers are usually grandmothers, siblings, or aunts and remain in that child's life going forward. If a child is unfamiliar with her caregivers or her caregivers are not emotionally available, separation is more difficult, and the results often have serious consequences for children.

Presence Means Teaching Guilt Without Shame

Your toddler is exploring the world with newfound motor skills, intense curiosity, and a push toward independence. She is struggling to internalize structure that the adults around her seem to insist on. It is an exciting time for secure mothers and infants, but a tense time too, and all the more tense if a mother is absent emotionally, very controlling, or fearful and ambivalent about her baby's newfound freedom. Think of infancy as the Garden of Eden: There are no rules, you can do what you want when you want to, and you don't feel badly about any of your behavior or desires. Then someone tells you that you have to follow rules, feel badly when you behave badly, and even be aware of your naked body and what other people think about it.

Feeling guilty is a necessary part of your child's emotional and social development. I want to make the distinction between shame and guilt. Shame occurs early in a child's life; it has to do with feelings of lovability and self-worth or value. Guilt occurs as children become self-aware and relates to socially appropriate behavior. Guilt, in moderate doses, is a useful tool for teaching and civilizing your toddler; shame creates a lack of connection and a sense of being alone, or abandoned. Note that I said *moderate* doses of guilt. The goal is to help your child develop a sense of self-discipline; you want her to feel badly enough about what she did to change her behavior, not badly ashamed of who she is. Harsh criticism from a parent can become harsh self-criticism and low self-esteem in an older child and adult.

Teaching your toddler to obey rules and respect boundaries is a balancing act. It requires patience and self-control on your part, and the ability to regulate your own emotions while your toddler is trying to master hers. Saying no to a toddler is like waving the proverbial red flag in front of a bull. I suggest to parents that a hard no be used only when there's an issue of health and/or safety at stake. For example, if your toddler reaches for a pair of scissors say, "No, that is sharp and that can hurt you, we don't play with scissors," and gently but firmly take the scissors away from her. But when health and safety are *not* an issue, try (difficult as it may be) to understand what your toddler is feeling and reflect it back to her, as you did when she was an infant, and show by your example what the right way to behave is. If your child throws her sippy cup full of juice, try saying, "I know it's fun to throw your sippy cup, but if you drop your cup the juice will spill out and you won't have any more juice. There will be a mess we have to clean up, and you might be sad, so let's not throw the sippy cup anymore."

Presence Means Reassuring Your Child at Night

Nighttime reassurance and security are essential to raising emotionally healthy and secure children, noted Elizabeth Higley and Mary Dozier, of the department of psychology at the University of Delaware.[15] It may be small comfort if your baby will sleep only an hour or two at a time. This is especially true of newborns, who must be fed every few hours until their stomachs grow and they can go for longer periods of time between feedings.

While many mothers in some other countries would not consider sleeping apart from their babies, in the United States most

babies have their own room. A family bed, or co-sleeping, is controversial at best and considered dangerous at worst. However,
mammals, including humans, evolved to sleep next to their infants,
and there are benefits for both mother and child when they sleep together for up to six months to a year. When a baby sleeps near her
mother she sleeps more soundly, is able to nurse on demand (if her
mother is breastfeeding) without waking completely (and without
her mother fully waking too), stays warmer without overheating, and
cries less. According to a study by David Waynforth, babies who co-
slept with their mothers had lower levels of cortisol.[16] Another study,
by R. Beijers, J. M. Riksen-Walraven, and C. de Weerth, and yet another by Wiesenfeld, et al., found that mothers who breastfed were
less anxious.[17] If the baby wakes, it's easier for both mother and child
to get back to sleep. If you're concerned about sleeping in the same
bed with your baby, consider using a bassinette or co-sleeper that at-
taches to your bed.

When your baby sleeps in his own room and cries for you, you have
to wake (more or less) fully and get out of bed. Lifting the baby out of
his crib to feed or change him stimulates him, and makes it harder for
him (and you) to go back to sleep.

In addition, babies are born with an upside-down sleep schedule.
As a pregnant woman lies down at night, her baby wants to party. This
makes sense when you realize that when a mother is at rest more blood
is available to her child. When a baby is born, she keeps the same
sleep–wake schedule, resting during the day and being more active at
night. We spend the weeks after birth helping adjust our baby's
schedule so she sleeps at night and is more active during the day. Your
baby is still most ready to interact at night when you want to sleep. At
night, your baby knows she doesn't have to compete for your attention
with chores, other people, or your cell phone. Why wouldn't she want
to stay up?

As your baby gets older, she will still be quite unsettled at night; nighttime is a time of separation from you, her main source of comfort. Is it any wonder she doesn't want to go to sleep until she's so tired she just collapses? Even if your baby is a good sleeper, you will find that she may not want to go to bed without you when she is upset or if you have been gone for a long time.

When your child cries for you in the middle of the night, remember he is crying because he is afraid. Go to him quickly and soothe him, using touch and your voice, or picking him up if necessary. Stay until he is able to fall back to sleep or until he is comfortable with your leaving; in this way you let him know that he is safe. Ignoring your baby's cries, or letting him cry to hysteria or vomiting, may teach him to fall asleep by himself in the short term, but may have long-term consequences for his emotional health. See Appendix C for some strategies that may help you and your child.

Special Advice for Working Mothers

Whether they work part or full time, working mothers on average have less time to spend with their children than nonworking mothers. They may find their child has more difficulty with transitions and sleep, and they spend as much (or more) time comforting their child as playing. Most working mothers feel tired, overwhelmed, conflicted, and guilty about not spending enough time with their children or devoting enough energy to their job, emotionally and physically depleted, and underappreciated. If you're a working mother, it may sometimes feel as if you have gotten more of the hard parts of motherhood than the sweet parts.

The best job for a working mother is one that offers control over how many hours she works and the flexibility to determine what those hours are. Whether or not you have the ideal job situation, there are options you can pursue that are in the best interests of your child and your family. If you have a job that requires shift work, whether you are a medical professional or a salesperson, day shifts are better than night shifts. If you must travel, day trips that allow you to be home for transition times, especially in the first three years, are better than those that require an extended stay. It is important to set boundaries about your work, both what your colleagues can expect from you and what you can expect from yourself.

Mara was able to strike a balance between her commitment to her children and her commitment to her work. A partner at a law firm, Mara negotiated a six-month maternity leave after the birth of her daughter and returned to work three days a week. When her son was born two years later, she cut back her work time to two days per week after she returned from leave, and still works part-time now that her children are in high school. Her position and tenure at the firm gave her an advantage when it came to negotiating both her leaves and work schedule. She says, "I definitely gave up a big promotion, money, and prestige, but I felt it was a fair trade-off to be with my children. And I have a closer relationship with my kids now that they are teenagers."

"I was honest with my employer and with myself—about what I could and could not do. I knew my boundaries and limitations, and expressed them explicitly. I knew myself, and what was important to me. I come from a family where there was such emphasis on nurturing and family that it was obvious to me what I valued above everything else, and that was relationships."

Mara is a good example of how important it is to embrace compromise not as an obligation, but as freedom. It is critical to know yourself and what is most important to you and to be realistic about what you can and cannot do and what you can and cannot have financially to remain present for your children. It is also important to be honest with your employer with your limitations and priorities. Presence is about self-knowledge, honesty, and, most important, about compromise.

> Presence is about self-knowledge, honesty, and, most important, about compromise.

Of course, everything I've said in this chapter applies to working mothers, but here are some tips to make it a bit easier for women who try to balance a career with raising a young child.

- Leave at least two hours between your return home and your baby's bedtime. If your baby has not seen you all day and you try to put her to bed as soon as you return, she will fight sleep.

- Be flexible about schedules, particularly around bedtime. If you come home later than usual, sit in your child's room with him until he falls asleep. You can calm and relax your child with soothing repetition: "It's time to sleep: Mommy is here." Or "It's nighttime and it's time to sleep and rest your body. Mommy is here." No matter what your mantra is, always include the phrase, "Mommy is here." You don't have to (and in fact should not) play or interact with your child when he is transitioning from wake to sleep. It's your presence and reassurance that your child needs. This can be your time to relax and even meditate. Think of it as a relaxing exercise rather than a burden and whatever you do don't put your child to bed if you are hungry, which will create a sense of urgency to get your child to sleep.

- Remember that nighttime security is even more important than daytime security. If you have been gone all day, expect your child to need you more at night and to wake more often.

> **Nighttime security is even more important than daytime security.**

- If you have more than one child, stagger bedtimes by ten or fifteen minutes so that each child can have time alone with you.

- Make it clear to your child through your actions that she, not work, is your priority. Keep your work life separate from your home life as much as possible. Be clear when you will respond to after-hours emails or calls. If you have to work at home at night or on a weekend, wait until your child is asleep for the night or is napping.

- Make your child rather than your significant other your priority when you return from work. Your partner can wait; your baby cannot.

- Do your best to keep regular hours. Even a very young baby will develop a sense of when their mother will be home and will get upset or sad when she doesn't arrive at the expected time.

- If you work from home, make allowances for having a more disrupted day. If you have an important call with a client or need

uninterrupted time to work on a report, arrange for your caregiver to take your child for a walk or to an activity.

- Spend as much time with your baby as you can. If you have
  been gone all day, try not to schedule an evening appointment.
  Your child's first three years is not the time to take a long vacation without him or to take a job that involves long business
  trips.

- Avoid coming home during the day if you have to leave immediately. Remember, once out and once in is best.

- If your budget allows, outsource as much housework and food
  preparation as possible or else try to do cleaning and meal prep
  when the baby is asleep. Online delivery services are available
  for everything from food to household goods to baby supplies.
  Use them. You can set up automatic delivery for things you buy
  every week.

- Use your commuting time and lunch hour for errands and other
  tasks, like paying bills.

- Say no to outside demands on your time as often as you can. The
  consequences usually aren't as dire as you imagine.

- Be conscious of your ambivalent feelings about work and parenting. Discuss your feelings with your spouse, your friends, or a
  therapist.

- Most important: Ask for help whenever you need it from
  whoever will help you!

Whether you stay home with your child or work outside the home, small changes in the way you handle distractions, transitions, and the time you spend *together* can make all the difference to your relationship.

Special Advice for Single Mothers

It's the rare single mother who does not have to work to support her children. She may often feel isolated and alone. At the end of the day, a single mother is often alone with her child when she returns home from work. She may not be able to be with her child for the important daily transitions. Single mothers need even more support than stay-at-home or working mothers who have partners; if she's sick, if the baby is sick, or when she is just plain exhausted, she usually has no one to step in and offer her relief. Without a partner or spouse, it's especially important for single mothers to build a village of family, friends, and neighbors they can rely on for support and who will share in the joys and challenges of childcare responsibilities.

If you are a single mother and have the resources and the space, the best option for both you and your child is to create a co-parenting situation with a live-in caregiver or family member. When you share the care of a child, you lean into your care partner to give you support so you can call on your emotional resources to care for your child. Mothers need nurturing themselves so they can nurture their children. When they are deprived of that support, it is harder for them to care for their children. That nurturing can come from multiple people: from your extended family and friends to your surrogate caregiver. The next best option to live-in support is a live-out caregiver (related or not) who will come to your home. For other options, see Chapter 6. No matter what arrangements you make for childcare, it's best to find a caregiver who will spend time with both you and your child at the beginning and end of your day to ease that transition, in addition to caring for your child while you are at work.

Consistency of care is particularly important for the children of single mothers; your caregiver (or caregivers) should be a presence in your child's life for as long as possible. If you can, arrange your work hours and other obligations around your child's schedule. However many hours you work, keeping a regular and predictable schedule will help your child feel secure.

And always remember, you and your baby are your first priority.

CHAPTER 5

Making It Better

Strengthening and Repairing the Mother–Child Bond

By the time they're three, children understand that you will return when you leave. Until that time, they live in the present and experience their separations from you as a loss; the younger the child, the more intense the feeling of loss. Even if you've been gone for only an hour or two, your absence frays the mother–child bond just a little, just as pulling on a sweater weakens the garment until it tears. The same thing happens when you misread a baby's distress during the course of a day. These pulls in the sweater of the mother and baby fabric are normal and expected. It is when you, as a present mother, are able to repair the upset from those miscues and absences that you make the fabric of your relationship stronger.

Moment-to-Moment Emotional Repair

Mothering is a moment-to-moment process of helping children regulate their emotions. Of course mothers cannot be present every moment of their child's first three years, whether they work outside the home or not, and even the most securely attached baby and mother miscommunicate almost half the time. When mother and baby are very connected to one another and in sync emotionally, the frayed fabric of the relationship is repaired quickly, before it becomes a tear.

> Mothering is a moment-to-moment process of helping children regulate their emotions.

Repairing the mother–child bond is essentially a team effort that begins with you. If you make the effort to repair your physical separation or emotional miscommunication with your child quickly and sensitively, then he feels heard and understood. Not only does this provide him with immediate comfort, but as those interactions are repeated, he learns he can depend on you and that he can self-soothe or distract himself until you are available. This security can be transferred to other caregivers and eventually other relationships, as he internalizes the understanding that, although others may not always understand what he needs every moment, he can handle such misunderstandings until his needs are met. This process reminds me of the 3-D printer in my daughter's school, which lays down, layer on layer, the object it's programmed to build until the object is complete. In this case, the object is the developing emotional self of the child. As a child's mother repairs another misattunement of emotion, she lays down another important layer of what will be that child's perception of how intimate relationships either meet your needs or don't.

A baby signals that he wants his mother by reaching, cooing, fussing, crying, or frowning. If you don't respond, he'll focus on an object or a part of his body like his fingers or toes. He may rock his body, or suck on his fingers or clasp his hands. If there's still no response, the baby may become listless, and become uninterested in his surroundings. Eventually he may literally turn away from his mother and lose the ability to maintain focus on something or someone else.

Ed Tronick, a developmental and clinical psychologist and associate professor of pediatrics at Harvard University who specializes in repairing the communication missteps between mothers and babies, observed, "The infant who employs coping strategies unsuccessfully and repeatedly fails to repair mismatches . . . begins to feel helpless . . . [and] eventually gives up attempting to repair the mismatches."[1] Tronick came to this conclusion by conducting experiments in which, for a few minutes at a time, mothers remained "still faced," or expressionless, in their babies' presence, much like a distracted, uninterested, depressed, or exhausted mother might. At first the babies tried to win their mothers over with smiles and vocalizations. When that got no response, they showed the signs of stress and rejection I listed earlier. When an infant has little impact on her mother's response, then despair sets in. In a study of seven-month-olds, Tronick also found that those mothers who were more positive with their infants had more playful and positive infants, whereas the babies of mothers who were depressed were less interested in playing or being social.[2]

This is how moment-to-moment repair looks:

Amanda's six-month-old daughter, Jennifer, has just woken up from a nap. She sits on the floor across from her mother. Amanda makes eye contact with Jennifer and speaks quietly to her daughter, easing the transition from sleep to play: "You're just waking up, and you want to play with Mommy, but you are still a little sleepy." Jennifer smiles and Amanda gently smiles in return. Amanda touches Jennifer's hand and Jennifer clasps her mother's hand and smiles and giggles. Amanda gets distracted by the buzz of her phone and turns away from her daughter, who frowns and fusses. Amanda turns back toward Jennifer, and says, "I'm sorry! I didn't pay attention to you." Jennifer reaches out to Amanda with arms outstretched and a smile and giggles. Amanda sings to Jennifer, and they look at a colorful book of nursery rhymes, but soon Jennifer needs a break and looks away at her toes in great fascination. Amanda calmly waits until Jennifer turns her attention back to the book; as in a chess game, she waits for her partner to make the next move before she rushes in to make her own move.

The pause between our interactions is a very important part of being present, but even more important for repairing misunderstandings in communication. When you are speaking with another adult, do you wait for your partner to finish his thoughts? Do you interrupt, or do you allow for the space between interactions to show respect for his opinions and feelings? By waiting for Jennifer to return to engage her, Amanda truly reflects her baby's feelings and where she is emotionally.

This subtle and nuanced repair of the comings and goings of social engagement and emotional regulation occurs all day long in the life of a baby. This dance of comfort, play, and responsiveness is how babies learn to navigate the world of their feelings.

The First Moments of Your Return

When your baby has spent time away from you in the care of others, the most important part of repair is how quickly it occurs after your reunion; I cannot stress this enough. As Mary Ainsworth's Strange

Situation Experiment demonstrated, what happens in the first moments of your return are both diagnostic and instructive about your
and your baby's relationship;[3] reading your baby or toddler's cues accurately after a physical and/or emotional separation is the key.
Whether you've been gone for much of the day or have run out to the
gym or the market, be open to whatever emotions she expresses, positive and not so positive. If you are willing to accept and acknowledge
that she may be sad or angry with you and may even want nothing to
do with you, you are much more likely to repair the rift caused by the
separation.

When mothers ask me if their baby reacting to them leaving or returning is a terrible thing, I tell them to be concerned if their baby has
no reaction or too intense a reaction, but do not worry if he has a reaction. Having *some* reaction—joy, excitement, anger, sadness—to
separation is normal and healthy and means your baby is attached to
you and feels the loss of your presence.

Repair after you have been away requires that you put aside everything else when you return. *Anything* that will distract you on your
return—a call you have to make, checking in with your spouse or
partner, even a trip to the bathroom—should all be put on hold when
you walk in the door and your eyes meet your baby's eyes for the first
time after you have been separated. You know the scene in romantic
movies of two lovers running toward each other with arms outstretched? Nothing so dramatic may happen when you return home,
yet to your baby, her great love has returned home, and it is a big
deal . . . or it should be!

If the greeting isn't all hugs and kisses, remember that your baby
may feel conflicted about your return. The conversation inside a securely attached baby's head may go something like this: "You left me
and you didn't come back right away and now you are back and I am
mad at you, but I need you, but you made me feel so sad today, but I

want you, are you back for good now or are you going to leave again, should I trust you, I don't know, oh hell, I have missed you, Mommy, give me a big hug and don't leave again!"

The conversation inside an insecurely attached baby's head might go something like this, "You left me like you always leave me and I am really mad at you, I don't trust you anymore and I can take care of myself, not really, but I know I can't trust you, let's see if there is anyone else I can trust who can take care of me, oh yeah, the babysitter is around more; I don't need you anymore." Or this: "Mommy, I have needed you so much today and you weren't here, where were you, I was so alone, I feel so empty without you don't ever leave me, Mommy please let me hold you and never let go, Mommy I have been so sad without you, come here and don't let me go."

Your baby's relationship to you is, in some ways, not much different from an adult romantic relationship. One of the first questions I ask when someone comes to me because of relationship difficulties is, "How do you feel when your partner goes away? Do you miss him or her?" If the answer is no, then either there is no love there, or my patient has trouble loving. It is the same for babies. If a baby has no reaction when reunited with his mother, it is often a sign of an attachment insecurity, not a healthy independence and self-reliance. On the opposite end of the spectrum, if a baby is hysterical upon separation and reunion, it's also a sign of insecurity and a rift in the fabric of the relationship with the mother that has not been adequately repaired.

Giving Your Child All of Your Attention

Putting aside the time after work as belonging to your child is important, particularly if you have been away for much of the day. I often recommend that mothers and fathers put their phones and all technology away in a basket near the front door that they don't touch until their children are asleep. That way there is no temptation to focus on their work or their social lives outside the family.

Suniya Luthar and Sean Latendresse's study of the children of affluent and poor parents found that the children who were the most emotionally healthy were the ones whose parents fell in the middle of the socioeconomic spectrum.[4] This may be because there was less pressure on both the parents and children to compete and succeed in everything, but more important, the parents had fewer demands for their time and attention.

> Xiomara, a single mother with three young children, came to the United States from Colombia. She found full-time work at a factory and made it clear to her children how much she missed them and wished she didn't have to leave them to go to work. When she came home, her time was her children's time, and she would not leave them again. Her job didn't bleed into her time at home, and she made it clear to her friends that if they wanted to see her they would have to include her children.

We know that financial stress and hardship, substandard and uncomfortable living conditions, and unfulfilling work are the kinds of stressors that impact parent–child relationships, but few people make the connection that great financial resources and ambition (either socially or professionally) are also conditions that can fracture that bond. When a mother comes home from work only to go out again for a dinner, her leaving so soon unravels whatever repair she has been able to implement with her baby.

Nighttime Repair Is Essential to Attachment Security

Nighttime is the scariest part of the day for children. Nighttime repair is critical for all mothers and children, but particularly for mothers who work or who are gone for more than an hour or two of the day. Many mothers from other cultures, Judi Mesman told me, find the American way of forcing children to sleep separately at such a young age and to cry it out as abuse. In our society's glorification of autonomy, we have idealized Ferber and his promotion of nighttime independence and, in doing so, have lost sight of the most important time we have to repair our emotional or physical absence. In a study on nighttime security, Elizabeth Higley and Mary Dozier found that a mother's sensitivity in responding to her child at night can make the difference between a secure and an insecure child.[5] In a study of mothers and children who lived on a kibbutz (a communal living situation in which both parents work full time and children are cared for in a group setting), Dr. Marinus van IJzendoorn, of Leiden University, found that babies who slept with their parents and whose mother comforted them during the night were more securely attached than those children who slept apart from their parents and whose mothers were not available to them.[6]

Nighttime is the time for mothers to repair the separations and misattunements of the day, through bodily contact, affection, and a speedy and sensitive response to their baby's fears.

Repair and Rebalancing

Repair may take the form of spending more time with your baby while holding down a job, but it also may mean taking a break from work or rethinking your work–family balance when your child is very young.

Repair often requires rebalancing priorities and responsibilities within a relationship. It may mean that the partner or spouse who is

not the primary caregiver has to take on more of the financial responsibility for the family for a short time, which may mean a change in
lifestyle. I often see fathers who may not understand the importance
of a mother's role and are fearful and unsupportive when their wives
want to cut back their work hours or want to stay at home with their
babies, particularly if this change threatens the financial status of the
family. Some feel betrayed because they married a woman who declared early on "I always want to work," but when she had a baby her
desire to care for her baby became her primary concern.

> Gina worked full time for a medical supply company and had
> told her husband she would always work. She went back to her
> job after a three-month maternity leave after each of her
> children. She came to see me when her daughter was three
> years old and her son was eighteen months old because she was
> worried about her daughter, who seemed angry at her all the
> time, and was hitting and kicking other children at daycare.
> Gina felt disconnected from her children, and felt she spent
> too little time with them. She recognized that to be present
> and to repair the distance between her and her children would
> mean quitting her job. Gina thus decided it was best for her
> children that she be at home full time and once she made the
> change, she was surprised to realize she felt far less stress, even
> though the family's financial situation changed and her
> husband was unhappy with her decision.
>
> With Gina's presence and attention, her daughter became
> less angry at her mother, and began to express her feelings
> with words rather than through physical aggression. Gina's
> son, who had seemed to adjust to his mother's absence during
> work hours, became noticeably more affectionate. Gina had
> no regrets about quitting her job and felt it was the best de-

cision she made, even with the strain it put on her marriage. Though her husband still struggled with her decision, he came to realize that, in spite of the change in their financial status, it was better for their children. Two years after she left her job, Gina decided to go back to work part-time.

I often find when I speak to young adults, particularly young women, that they believe what they tell their boyfriends, fiancés, and young husbands: "I will always work full-time, so basically nothing will change in my life or yours when we have children." Well, someone didn't get the memo! *Everything* changes when you have children. I always tell young women never to make these kinds of promises. A young, single full-time mother said to me, "I don't know how women who work and have husbands can be present for their babies, it is hard enough when you don't work and don't have a spouse to deal with." Never a truer statement was made.

It might sound controversial, but it's really just basic common sense: There are a finite number of hours in the day, and your energy levels and emotional resources can be stretched only so far. If you have a very demanding career or if your husband is not very supportive of you having or caring for children, then you are setting up a situation of competing needs, and there will be less of you for your children.

It is normal for partners to have some resentful and competitive feelings about the mother's or primary caregiver's connection to their baby in the first three years, but the hard truth is that your partner will need to make some sacrifices, some emotional and some physical (hello, lack of sleep), when your child is very young. If this competition is very intense and remains an unresolved conflict, it can impact the relationship both you and your partner have with each other and with your child.

How do you deal with a spouse who doesn't support your time and presence with your baby at the end of the day? Your knowledge and self-confidence regarding the fact that your baby needs you will be the bridge to your spouse's acknowledgment and acceptance. When your partner understands how important the first three years of your child's life is to her health and future, it may help him or her adjust more easily to the changes in your relationship. And I always remind fathers that they play a critical role in nurturing their children, if they can just be patient and support the mother in the present.

And what happens if you have other children who are demanding your attention too when you come home? Repair with siblings means helping them understand the concept of taking turns with Mom. When your other children are under the age of three it's like trying to tell them they should share a toy with each other. It can seem impossible to share a toy, just as it is impossible to share a mother's love and attention. It is more realistic to tell a child to take turns with the toy.

It's best that each child has a separate reunion with you. The younger the child, the greater her need for immediate reunion on your return. One way to deal with this is to call your caregiver or partner and arrange for your older child to meet you outside or just inside the door, giving him the "prize" of having your attention first. You can then turn your attention to your baby. After they are three years old, children are able to more easily share your attention with their younger siblings until you can spend some time alone with them.

Remember, there are only so many ways of slicing the pie of your attention. Forget the idea of quality time; the more real physical time you have with your child, the more chances there are for moments of connection. And of course the less time you have, the harder it is to force the connection to your child on your terms.

Therapy and Reflection Are Repair

Reflection is required for repair. But most important, repair begins with yourself first as a mother before you even engage your baby. Mothers have to repair the feelings of unresolved loss, sadness, and anger about their own mothers before they can hope to repair the rift with their babies when they are unavailable, whether for a moment or for a day. Although I am giving you some direction, suggestions, and advice, all of this is useless unless you can dig deep inside yourself to understand your desire for, or fear of, connection, dependency, and intimacy. Most mothers would say they love their children and they want to be close to their children, but on deeper reflection many realize there are serious emotional obstacles and conflicts that may interfere with their desire to be close to their babies.

Talk therapy, which is reflective, is the greatest form of repair. For some mothers, it may be the first time they feel someone understands them, which enables them to relate to their babies in a different way. Therapy provides mothers not only with a place to bring their feelings of anger, sadness, loss, and mourning but also a place to get support and help with intensifying their connection to their baby and with rebalancing their lives. Therapy provides the environment that allows a mother to look at her own internal conflicts as well as conflicts in her marriage while it supports a mother's decision to focus on the needs of her baby without foregoing her own.

The good news: it's never too late to begin the process of repair, for yourself and for your child.

> It's never too late to begin the process of repair, for yourself and for your child.

You're Doing the Best You Can

Often a mother has no options to work or not work, and the time she spends away from her children is not of her own choosing. For Xiomara, taking a job in a factory to support her three children was not her first choice, and her sadness and pain was evident when she spoke with me twenty-five years later. Her ability to talk to her children about their situation of need and the very hard decisions she had to make and her willingness to express her sadness then and now have been very big parts of the repair with her children. Even so, Xiomara could still feel the anger from her grown daughter, who felt that separation as a trauma, though her sons were able to forgive her.

When a child is separated from his mother, he is in his most vulnerable and fragile state of being; accepting this sadness helps both the baby and the mother mourn the loss. As we know from losing loved ones, if we do not mourn at the time of a loss, we suppress and internalize our feelings, only to feel them later—with a vengeance—or have them converted into physical and emotional symptoms that can be harder to treat. When we feel too guilty or uncomfortable with our absence or our child's feelings and either ignore or deny them, the discrepancy between the baby's feelings and our feelings makes a baby feel most alone. When we not only allow our babies to feel sad but also acknowledge their sadness both nonverbally and verbally, we are engaged in repair.

It's normal for a baby to feel anger as well as sadness when her mother leaves. If a baby cannot soothe herself or is not comforted by her caregiver, she may become angry, become physically aggressive, or sometimes show extreme behavior, like banging her head against a crib or throwing herself on the floor.

When a baby hits his mother when she goes away or returns, it is a sign that he feels angry at her for not being either physically or emotionally present enough. It is our ability to understand these feelings, accept them, and acknowledge them with our actions and our words that repairs the rift between us and our child. If you punish your child's aggression, retaliate nonverbally (by turning away or making an angry face) or verbally, or emotionally shut down because you are upset or feel rejected, then your baby essentially has no place that is safe to take his feelings.

Repair is about having a safe place where you and your baby can share and work through your feelings together. It requires an emotionally secure and empathic mother to accept her baby's sadness and aggression, and I realize it doesn't come naturally to all women and may be influenced by their own childhood experiences.

Openly and authentically expressing your sadness to your children over your absence—"I feel so sad when I am at work and can't be home with you"—is the first step in repairing the separation when you have been away. I believe that children have radar for their parents' unconscious feelings; they know when you are doing the best you can do and can feel when you are striving to be better. They know when you want to be with them more but cannot and can forgive you. However, children also know when mothers *do* have choices of some kind, and if you are often choosing other activities over them, they feel this too.

You must be able to forgive yourself for your time away from your child, particularly if you have few choices or if you need to step away to preserve and refuel so you can be more available to your baby. However, the most critical part of repairing your absence, whether for a few moments or a few hours, is to recognize and accept your child's feelings toward you when you leave and when you return. A mother said to me recently, "What I would have given if my mother had taken responsibility for her unavailability; if she had said sorry and meant it."

CHAPTER 6

When You Can't Be There

The Benefits and Challenges of Surrogate Caregiving

The best situation for your child is to have your physical and emotional presence for much of the time in the first three years. I know it is unrealistic for many women because of financial challenges, a strong desire to be engaged in work outside the home, or emotional obstacles. If you can't care for your baby yourself, the next best option is individual surrogate care, whether it is your husband or partner, your mother or other relative, or a nanny. If that is not feasible, sharing a caregiver with another family can be a cost-effective option. I believe the least good option for surrogate care is daycare or institutional care, but if you use daycare, you'll find suggestions for choosing one that will provide the best experience for your child.

Some in my field believe it is better for a woman who does not feel as if she is patient enough or isn't good with children to leave her baby with a better surrogate. I don't believe that we should give up on the critical mother–baby relationship so quickly. This does not mean that a warm and loving surrogate is not helpful in supporting and relieving some of a mother's stress, but when the surrogate takes the conflict away and when society tells mothers that it is better for someone else to raise her baby because she is struggling and conflicted, then Houston, we have a problem. This is the time the hard work with mothers should begin. This is the point of departure for many of the mothers I see who feel terrible guilt from leaving their babies. However, it is when these mothers flee that they often have the strongest feelings of guilt, and it is when their babies need them most that they take this path. This is the point at which a community of pediatricians, nurse practitioners, therapists, and parent guidance experts should be stepping in to support these mothers, helping them get to the bottom of their conflicts and be more available to their babies rather than less available.

Who Is a Primary Caregiver?

Speaking at a conference on attachment, Margaret Mahler, a developmental psychoanalyst who advanced the theory of separation-individuation in children, defined a *primary caregiver* as "the person who cares for the baby throughout the day."[1] Because a baby's physical and emotional health are deeply connected, a primary caregiver is critical to the emotional development and mental health of a child. It is the primary caregiver a baby turns to when she feels frightened, worried, or needs reassurance or comfort when she is in distress. A primary caregiver provides the nurturing that allows a child to develop into a secure, loving, emotionally competent individual. In most parts of the world this is the mother.

Today fewer women in Western societies are taking this role, leaving the day-to-day care of their infants in the hands of others. A 2012 study by the U.S. Department of Labor found that one in four new mothers were back at work within just two weeks of giving birth. College graduates took the longest leaves, but that usually meant only six weeks. Those without a degree (54 percent) were able to stay home for only a week or two,[2] which simply is not enough time for mother and child to form a secure bond.

However long a mother works or needs time away from her baby, she must share the care of her child with other caregivers. In many countries, particularly in the developing world, children have multiple caregivers; this is called alloparenting. These caregivers are usually grandmothers, aunts, close neighbors, or siblings, all of whom are invested in the well-being of the child and will be with her throughout her life. In this model of care, said Judi Mesman, "The mother is still the center of attachment for the baby, and is present while the baby is handed from one member of the family to another. So when the baby needs to touch base with his mother for security she is right there." This is in contrast to the Western model, in which mothers leave their child in the care of others and are physically and emotionally unavailable for hours. Unfortunately, as economies change, the Western model of outsourcing childcare is taking root in other parts of the world. On a recent trip to South Africa, Dina, a mother of two who worked in a childcare center for working mothers, told me, "It used to be that your mother and relatives helped to care for your baby, now you don't know who is caring for them and you have to leave them in the care of strangers."

The alloparental model is very different from the prevailing early childcare model in the United States, where parents rely less on family and more on group daycare or a nanny or babysitters. Almost one-quarter of children under the age of five are in some kind of organized care, like daycare or preschool. Western mothers are also more likely to leave their infants and young children for longer periods of time as they return to work and other activities. A child may have multiple sitters over the course of her first three years, what I call a revolving door of caregivers, rather than a familiar and consistent group of caregivers.

We know that babies mourn the loss of their mothers, even when they're separated for a few hours. When we don't acknowledge that loss, there is a big elephant in the emotional and physical room in which the baby lives. Even when adopted children have loving parents, they still are curious about and often seek out their biological mothers. To ignore this very real need in children denies our most basic biological instincts. Does this mean that a father or a man or woman who is not biologically connected to a child cannot be a present caregiver? Or that a babysitter cannot provide loving care? Of course, all of these relationships are possible, but only if we first recognize a few important things. It is critical to recognize the primacy and importance of a child's biological mother, even if that woman is not raising him. It is important to acknowledge that the best-paid surrogate caregiver will not be as invested in a child as is a relative. Only when whoever is taking the place of the mother (for no matter how long) can be sad with a child and acknowledge the feelings of loss, rather than denying that they exist, can he or she help him move from mourning to acceptance. This can be as simple as verbally acknowledging those feelings and responding, "I hear you miss Mommy. Maybe we can be sad together before we go and play."

When a Father Is the Primary Caregiver

Though more and more fathers are taking on the role of primary caregiver to their children, traditionally, mothers and fathers have played different roles in caring for the emotional needs of their babies. Mothers have provided emotional regulation and balance, and, most important, the downregulation or calming and soothing of the nervous system. They have been the objects of attachment and security as well as touching, affection, soothing, and comfort, particularly when a baby is in distress. Fathers have provided primarily playful stimulation and have been important in helping babies separate from their mothers when they are ready to explore the world of play and independence.

Although there are some fathers who are more sensitively nurturing than some mothers, in general there is a difference in their styles of nurturing; mothers and fathers are *not* exactly the same. Research shows this is the result of the different levels of hormones produced by men and women. As mentioned earlier, mothers produce the neurotransmitter oxytocin when they give birth and breastfeed, which is responsible for the empathic nurturing a mother shows her baby or toddler. Fathers produce more vasopressin, a neurotransmitter that produces a more aggressive protective response. Mothers produce some vasopressin too, but vasopressin is most connected to testosterone (which also influences aggression as well as the drive to reproduce), while oxytocin is more connected to estrogen. When men spend more time with their children, their balance of hormones changes: They produce more oxytocin. James Rilling, at Emory University, found that when men produce more oxytocin, their levels of testosterone decrease, and they become more like present mothers in how they nurture their children.[3]

Mark and his wife, the provost of a Midwestern university, wanted their children to have the experience of a full-time stay-at-home parent; her salary was substantially higher than Mark's, and he was less involved in his job, so the decision that he should become the primary caregiver was a relatively easy one. His sons are now four and six, and he is the parent they run to when they want to be comforted, and the parent who responds when one of the children wakes up in the middle of the night. He feels that being the parent his children are closest to and with whom they share the important details of their lives is deeply rewarding work. While Mark has always been warm and approachable, he consciously modeled his caregiving behavior on the example of his mother and mother-in-law. He also found John Gottman's book *Raising an Emotionally Intelligent Child* extremely helpful.

Dr. Ruth Feldman, from Bar Ilan University in Israel, has done research on the differences in maternal and paternal nurturing. Mothers, who produce oxytocin naturally or are given additional oxytocin, engage in more touching, eye contact, and calm play. Fathers who are given oxytocin do interact with their babies more than before, mostly through physical and stimulating (or what some mothers may consider rough) play, like throwing them up in the air and catching them.[4] Babies need both calm and excitement, which makes a strong argument for a child's need for both a mother and a father. While it may be instinctive for a father to try to distract or jolly a child when she is crying, what the child needs is something else. Many fathers, especially those who are not primary caregivers, do not respond to baby's cries with the same speed or level of comforting care as mothers (as any woman who has been woken in the middle of the night by her child's cries, while her husband slept soundly, knows). A study at the University of Sussex showed that fathers are, however, disturbed by soft nature sounds, like buzzing flies or chirping crickets, and by the sound of a loud wind moving through the bushes.[5] David Lewis, a neuropsychologist, suggested that "These differing sensitivities may represent evolutionary differences that make women sensitive to sounds associated with a potential threat to their children, while men are more finely tuned to disturbances posing a possible threat to the whole family."[6] A father who is the primary caregiver needs to understand that during a child's first year of life, what is most important, even essential, is responding to and comforting his child *quickly and sensitively* when she is distressed.

It's not unusual to have one parent who is warmer and more empathic while the other takes a stricter, let-him-cry-it-out approach, for example, and just as with a hired caregiver, a consistent approach to caring for your child is best. Especially in the first year of your child's life, it's important for a father to become more sensitive to his child's cries and signals of distress and respond as quickly as possible whether he is a stay-at-home dad or not.

Agreeing on a division of household responsibilities is essential. Who handles paying the bills? Doing the laundry? Cleaning the bathroom? The grocery shopping? Who takes care of making doctors' appointments and playdates? When you come home, are you taking over care of your child? What about weekends?

It is also critical that you agree to address issues of jealousy and competition. A baby's strongest attachment to a parent is usually to the one who spends the most time with her. She is more likely going to choose her father when she needs a cuddle if he has been cuddling her all day, and that can create feelings of jealousy and competiveness in you. Or if you come home and she immediately cries for you, your partner or spouse may become upset.

There are issues of balance of power and financial control in all marriages, but they can become more complicated when a father takes on a nontraditional role. These issues can extend into the bedroom; after money, the biggest area of disagreement between couples is intimacy and sex. As exhausted as you both may be, do not let these issues fester. The health of your marriage depends on both of you being able to talk about these uncomfortable topics. If testosterone goes down when oxytocin rises, the question of how this may impact men's sexual drive has yet to be answered by research.

It's a good idea for couples who choose for the father to be the primary caregiver to have these discussions before you have a child and to revisit them often. If you have serious differences in your approach to raising your family or concerns about how you and your partner or spouse will handle issues as they arise, consider going for parent guidance.

A number of my patients are gay male couples, and one of the first things I ask is which one of them is playing the role of *mother*. Often, they look at me as if I had three eyes, but in fact the question is an important one. It is preferable when raising a baby to have both a "mother" and "father," even if the mother is a man. If both parents are more comfortable with "father nurturing," that is exciting play and encouraging self-reliance, a baby may not get enough "mother nurturing," or sensitive nurturing and calming care. If two men are going to raise an emotionally healthy child (or children), one of them should take on the nurturing, empathic role.

If you are a stay-at-home dad raising your child while your wife, husband, or partner goes to work, there are certain things you can do to ensure that your child is getting what she needs emotionally:

- Empathic sensitive nurturing may not come naturally to you. This means leaning into a child's pain and not minimizing or dismissing her feelings. For instance, if your child falls down and skins her knee, instead of encouraging her to be brave and pick herself up, kiss her boo-boo and tell her you know how much it must have hurt. Then give her a hug and wait until *she* is ready to move on.

- Balance stimulating play with calmer play, like reading or arts and crafts. Practice putting your child's feelings into words and being with your child in a quieter, more reflective way.

- Accept and value all your child's feelings, including the sad, angry, and disappointed ones. Don't be afraid to talk about feelings.

- Focus on the details of your child's life rather than her overall well-being. Ask very specific questions. Instead of "Are you okay? Yes, great," try "Are you feeling sad because I had to go out for a little while to go to the supermarket?"

Choosing a Surrogate Caregiver

I believe that the alloparental model of care is the best for both mother and child. If you live near family or have connections to other maternal figures (long-time neighbors or family friends or "aunties"), explore whether they could be a source of support for you and might be willing to help with childcare.

Xiomara, whom you met earlier, would have left her children with her mother or sister when she lived in Colombia, but they had remained behind. In their place she hired a trusted friend who lived in the same apartment building, and left her children in her care. I realize that this is not always possible, either because of physical distance, or family conflict, but it's worth considering who in your trusted inner circle of loved ones, including close friends, is in a position to participate in your child's care.

In a society where family members often live far apart and may see each other only a couple of times a year, a hired nanny often replaces the experience of extended family helping raise children. The ideal surrogate caregiver is one who will care for your child as you would if you were there, will respect the unique bond between you and your child, and will promote that bond whenever you are present. This means that when you are away, this individual embraces the role of primary caregiver, and when you are home with your child, the surrogate will step back and yield that role to you. This is harder than you might think, for both of you.

I know that au pairs, young women from abroad who provide live-in childcare in return for room and board, are popular, especially in urban areas. I don't think they're the best choice for infants and very young children, for a number of reasons. Au pairs stay with a family for just a year, and often have little experience in caring for infants and young children. Because of their age, they often lack maturity and good judgment. If you want to bring in an au pair, it's best to wait until your children are five or six.

Think of your nanny as a more permanent connection to your child and you rather than a temporary one. A surrogate caregiver should be a *constant* in a child's life for as long as possible, but no matter how involved you get with your nanny and no matter how much your caregiver may love your child, the relationship is usually more temporary. It is important to keep your caregiver for as long as possible because the constant loss of surrogate caregivers can take a toll on a child's sense of security. After your caregiver leaves when you no longer need her, I encourage you to have as much contact with her as possible, as you would with a grandmother or aunt.

Choosing the right caregiver for your child requires that you be realistic about your situation. If you are away from home for fifty hours a week and your child is awake for only seventy hours a week, the surrogate will become the primary caregiver by default and may know your child better than you do. You may feel a combination of relief that your child is well taken care of, guilt that you are not with him more, and jealousy toward your caregiver for the relationship she has with your child, especially if your child will not let you comfort him and turns to his nanny instead. While this may be difficult for you, a caregiver who is emotionally involved with your child is providing an essential bond, and this relationship should be respected. Some mothers who feel threatened by the closeness between their caregiver and their child will hire a procession of nannies, rather than allow their child to develop a strong, secure bond with another person. Needless to say, this isn't in the child's best interest; a close and caring bond between caregiver and child is the goal, not something to be avoided (we'll discuss this more later in this chapter). Faced with a revolving door of caregivers, these children often become anxious, depressed, and/or distrustful of others or overly attached to strangers.

Just as you should never go food shopping when you are hungry, you don't want to hire a surrogate caregiver when you are in a rush or desperate. It's common for mothers to choose nannies who reflect their own mothering style. Think about what you enjoy and do well as a mother and also about what makes you uncomfortable. Your caregiver should not just support, but also complement and supplement your own approach. When you're interviewing a caregiver, consider her emotional intelligence as well as her practical skills and experience. She may have taken a course in first aid and CPR, but will she also give your child the affection and emotional nurturing that he needs? I suggest hiring a prospective caregiver for a trial day or two before you make a commitment so you can observe how the nanny relates and interacts with your child, and if your child feels safe with the nanny.

I am a co-founder of Nannies Who Know, a company that educates caregivers of young children to be more emotionally intelligent. Here are some of the things we look for in a caregiver and questions we suggest mothers ask when speaking with a prospective caregiver (for a more complete list of questions, see Appendix A):

- Does the caregiver make eye contact? Is she comfortable with touch when you shake her hand or put your hand on her shoulder?

- Why does she want to work with children? What is it about working with children she enjoys?

- Does she have children of her own? If she lights up when she talks about her children it's a good sign.

- Let her interact with your child. Does she engage her? How does she talk to her? If your child seems upset or fearful, does she try to soothe her or cheer her up? How does she do so?

- If your baby is asleep or calm during the interview, ask how she handles a baby who is in distress and crying, especially if he does not stop crying.

- How would she handle a toddler who is having a tantrum, one who is potty training and has an accident, or a child who is aggressive or angry?

- Does she like to play, and what kind of play does she enjoy with children?

- Ask her about her likes and dislikes. How does she communicate her feelings?

- Is she comfortable using the phone and computer (FaceTime, texting, Skype) to communicate with you while you're away?

- How does she feel about working while you're home?

- Does she see being a nanny as a profession or a temporary position? Make it clear when interviewing that you are looking for a long-term commitment and someone who will essentially become a member of your extended family, even after your professional relationship ends.

• Trust your feelings. If someone ticks all the boxes, but you don't feel comfortable, don't hire her.

Sharing the Care: Helping Your Child Adjust to Multiple Attachments

When you bring a new caregiver into your home, allow for a period of adjustment for your child. Spend as much time as possible with your child and her caregiver for at least two weeks (or until you feel that your child is comfortable with the new arrangements) so she can still use you as her security touchstone, gradually increasing the time she spends exclusively with her caregiver. This is also the time for you to show your caregiver how you want her to deal with comforting, feeding, discipline, naptime, and other aspects of your child's daily routine.

The key to helping your child adjust to a new caregiver is creating smooth transitions. This may require that you allow more time in your schedule so there's overlap between the time your caregiver arrives and you leave, and the time you arrive and your caregiver leaves. Whenever possible (even into adolescence), be present for at least two of the four big transition times: waking up, going to preschool, coming home from preschool, and bedtime, even when you have a wonderful, caring surrogate.

Your child looks to you for cues about whom to trust. Use your words and your body language to show your child how much you like and trust your caregiver. The more affection your child sees you show your caregiver, the more he will trust her too. Show your caregiver the courtesy and consideration you expect from another adult; talk about subjects other than your child and plan to share an occasional meal.

> The more affection your child sees you show your caregiver, the more he will trust her too.

If after a few weeks your child still has not found comfort in a caregiver's arms or her behavior changes, your child may be telling you that her connection with the caregiver is not working. Some regression is normal when a new caregiver comes into the home, but signs of a serious mismatch include sleep and eating disturbances, showing fear or anxiety when you leave or in the presence of your caregiver, developmental regression (such as increased trouble separating and potty training accidents in an older toddler), and loss of language if your child has begun speaking. Don't just hope that things will get better. Address your concerns with your caregiver, and if your child's distress continues, look for a new caregiver.

Competition Between Mothers and Surrogate Caregivers (Even When They Are Fathers)

It is quite common for mothers to feel threatened and ambivalent about their decision to give up being the primary caregiver, particularly when their baby becomes very attached to his babysitter, nanny, or father. Babies tend to be drawn to the person who provides them with the greatest presence and emotional and physical availability. If you have been gone for most of the day, when you return, it is not uncommon for your baby to seek the person who has been the source of his security throughout the day. When a mother cares for a baby all day and a father returns from work, fathers experience some of the same cold shoulder treatment from the baby.

It is normal to see *some* attachment to the nanny at the end of the day. In fact, as long as he hasn't rejected you, you want to see that your baby has attached to your nanny or partner—you want your alternative caregiver to be very connected to your child, and your child to his caregiver.

If you cannot be home with your child, the most generous choice you can make is to provide a warm, affectionate caregiver, rather than one who has a strict, "tough love" attitude. When a nonmaternal caregiver gets close to a baby it is a wonderful and complicated thing for many mothers. Sometimes mothers who are fearful of their child becoming too attached to an alternative caregiver will unconsciously choose an emotionally detached nanny or one who is more discipline-oriented than affectionate, feeling that she will be less competition for the child's affection.

I always encourage mothers to hire nannies who can mother them too. There was many a day when I lay in bed with a bad cold and our nanny brought me chicken soup or ginger tea. The more love and support you get as a mother, the more love and support you can give to your baby. If you don't feel your nanny cares for you, it will be hard for you to work as a team to care for your children.

If you are ambivalent about working or spending time away from your child, and even if you are comfortable and happy with your choice to have another caregiver, you may have a difficult time with your feelings of rejection, anger, sadness, guilt, or being competitive with your child's caregiver. This is completely natural, and these feelings should not be ignored or suppressed. It's fine to tell your caregiver that it makes you sad that your baby turns away from you when you come home or that you wish you could spend more time at home. When you think about and express your feelings, you begin to make sense of *why* you're feeling a particular way and also what you may want or need to do about it. If you don't recognize and acknowledge these emotional conflicts and feelings of competition with your surrogate caregiver, you may unconsciously act on them by finding fault with and ultimately dismissing her, which wouldn't be fair to you, her, and especially your child.

Fathers who stay home with their baby have a special challenge. There are, of course, the cultural and societal assumptions they have to deal with. They may feel that as the primary caregiver they deserve the "good stuff" of love and attachment at the end of the day and may not easily relinquish their role when a mother comes home. Even though a father has cared for the baby most of the day, when her mother returns, it is not unusual for a baby to cling to her mother, leaving the father to feel rejected or angry. Fathers may feel resentful that their baby seems to prefer her mother and mothers may feel resentful that the father seems to have a kind of intimacy with their baby that they have given up.

When a father agrees to be the primary caregiver he often is unaware of the conflicts that can create stress on a marriage. If your partner or spouse will be the primary caregiver in your home, you'll need to communicate honestly and often, not just about your child's needs but about your relationship and how reversing the traditional gender roles is affecting you both.

Practical Ways to Support Your Caregiver: Communication, Expectations, and Feedback

Having a good relationship with your surrogate caregiver is critical for the emotional well-being of your baby (and you), and a big part of that is open and frequent communication between the two of you.

If your caregiver is from another culture, open communication with an authority figure may not come naturally because it may be perceived as a sign of disrespect. Let your caregiver know you are not only okay with her honestly expressing her feelings and concerns to you but you consider it an essential part of the job.

Other things you can do to help make your relationship with your caregiver a healthy one:

- Be clear about what you expect from your caregiver. You cannot expect your nanny to know what you want or need in terms of your style and methods of caring for your child if you are not transparent and explicit. This should include how you want her to deal with all the physical aspects of your child's care—eating, clothing, napping, playing, toilet training—as well encouraging the emotional intimacy between her and your child.

- When you hire your nanny, provide her with a detailed job description that includes her responsibilities, schedules, pay, vacation, sick days, and any other benefits such as transportation or reimbursement for her cell phone. Give your nanny sufficient warning about schedule changes, a change in her responsibilities, or any aspect of the job.

- Be realistic about your expectations. Asking her to do light housekeeping is fine, but her first priority should be your child.

- Make eye contact with your caregiver when you speak with her and show interest in her life outside your home. Don't talk down to your nanny or speak in a harsh, condescending, or overly critical manner. How you treat your nanny is how they will treat your child. Be self-aware!

- Your caregiver may be worried about hurting your feelings if your child shows he's very attached to her. Reassure her that this is exactly the kind of relationship that you want them to have.

- Consider sending your nanny to a course on relating to your baby using emotional intelligence; it's also a great activity for mothers and nannies to do together.

- When you are away from home, speak to your nanny and your child throughout the day. Use FaceTime and Skype, which make visual as well as verbal communication possible.

- Remember that your nanny is doing the most important work there is—helping to nurture your most precious child. Treat her with affection and respect and let her know you appreciate what she does.

- Anger erodes relationships. It is inevitable that there will be conflicts regarding differences of opinions, schedules, honest mistakes, and conflicting individual needs. If there's a problem—your caregiver is consistently late, for example—address and resolve the problem as quickly as possible.

- Take the initiative and ask your nanny often how she is doing and how she feels the job is going. Let her know it's okay to express her concerns or negative feelings.

Make time for your caregiver in your day. Listen to what she has to say about your child; she may spend more time with him than you do. Sometimes nannies see things in families that you may be too close to see; if your child is having difficulty with your absence, for example. Listen without becoming defensive; if your caregiver brings issues like this to you and you react negatively she may be afraid to be open with you in the future.

The Problem with Daycare

Of all the options for alternative childcare for children under the age of two, daycare is the most problematic, and yet it is the most widely used method of childcare in the Western world. In an April 2013 article in the *New Republic*, "The Hell of American Day Care: An Investigation into the Barely Regulated, Unsafe Business of Looking After Our Children," Jonathan Cohn wrote: "American daycare is a mess. About 8.2 million kids—about 40 percent of children under five—spend at least part of their week in the care of somebody other than a parent. Most of them are in centers. . . . Excellent day cares are available, of course if you have the money to pay for them and the luck to secure a spot. But the overall quality is wildly uneven and barely monitored, and at the lower end, it's Dickensian."[7] And yes, unfortunately, it is as bad as described in many cases.

Daycare may be cost-effective (sometimes), but it is not the best choice for the health and well-being—and specifically the emotional development—of our children. It is the antithesis of the alloparental model of care: A mother leaves her child for long periods of time in the care of multiple strangers (rather than with one consistent and nurturing surrogate); there are too few caregivers for too many children; the caregivers are often transitory, rather than long term, and are too often poorly trained. The daycare environment is for the most part noisy, overstimulating, and overwhelming to a baby, whose nervous system is still developing. In addition to suffering from the loss of his mother, in many daycare situations a child is dealing with a series of constant losses as staff comes and goes.

And what kind of nurturing care can an overtaxed staff give? Each state has different criteria for an acceptable staff to child ratio. In California, the state permits one caregiver for four babies aged six weeks to nine months.[8] In Ohio, the ratio is one caregiver to five infants under the age of a year, or two caregivers for twelve infants if they're in the same room. For toddlers eighteen to thirty months, it's one caregiver to seven children; from thirty to thirty-six months, it's one caregiver to eight children.[9] How would you feel if you had to take care of four or five or six babies? Or seven toddlers? How would you handle diaper changes, feedings, naps? How much individual attention could you give each child? If they were all crying at the same time, how would you calm them? Would you become impatient or angry? Would you ignore the child or children who were hard to comfort? Even the most skilled and empathic caregiver finds caring for multiple babies at the same time a challenge.

Some people cite the benefits of early socialization when advocating for daycare. Socialization is an important part of growing up, but children aren't equipped psychologically or emotionally to be social in a group setting before the age of two. In fact, babies do not need group socialization at such a young age, but they *do* need a primary caregiver to make them feel safe. Drs. Alan Stein and Kathy Sylva, at Oxford University, discovered that a child's participation in group daycare before she is two increases the chance she will develop other behavioral issues later in childhood as a reaction to coping with her fear of abandonment and loss.[10] One of the ways this can manifest is in aggression and anger, and a premature independence (which, as discussed earlier, is not a good thing).

Not everyone has a mother or aunt who can pitch in or a spouse or partner who is willing to be a stay-at-home dad. Not everyone can afford to pay for a single full-time caregiver. A better option than institutional daycare, which can often be no more expensive, is sharing a caregiver with another family.

There are a number of advantages to this kind of arrangement, which is becoming popular in California (always a thought leader) and increasingly throughout the rest of the country:

- Research has shown us that for children under the age of two, the best ratio of caregiver to child is one to two or, at most, one to three.[11]

- Even if you alternate homes with the other family, your child will be in a calmer, more familiar environment, which makes the big transitions of your leaving and coming home less stressful.

- Multiple caregivers, especially when they move in and out of a child's life frequently, are upsetting for a baby. One shared caregiver is easier for your child to adjust to and is more likely to be with your family longer.

If daycare is your only option, your presence is even more important to your child when you are with her. Make sure you are the one to drop off and pick up your child. The more hours a child spends in daycare, the more important nighttime security and daily repair of the mother–child bond becomes. You'll find more information on this in Chapter 5.

To find the best daycare situation for your child, consider the following points:

- Make sure the facility is licensed, even if it's in someone's home.

- The more staff to children the better. One caregiver to two or three children is optimal.

- Will your child have a consistent primary caregiver or will multiple people care her for? The best option is that she is assigned a specific caregiver.

- Look for a mature, experienced, stable staff. Ask how long the staff has been there and what kind of training and certification they have received.

- Is the staff willing to talk with you about your child? If they brush off your concerns, or are unwilling to talk with you about your child's day, look for another care situation.

No matter what choice you make regarding alternative care for your child, you should do your best to minimize the time you spend away from him and maximize the time you are with him.

PART 2

THE COSTS OF BEING ABSENT

CHAPTER 7

Understanding the Costs
of Being Absent

The families I see in my practice come to me because there is something wrong. Sometimes a mother is depressed or unhappy and doesn't understand why. Sometimes she comes to me because she is concerned about her child's emotional state or his behavior at home or in school. Sometimes the parents come to me directly; often a school, a pediatrician, or daycare suggests a child needs help. While not every child's symptoms or conditions are related to a mother's absence or inattentiveness or a child's attachment problems, many *are* linked to a child's early experiences with his mother. My observations are confirmed by the research of Dr. Marinus van IJzendoorn.[1] I see issues such as anxiety (which shows itself as attention difficulties, aggression, and behavior issues), depression, social difficulties, lack of resilience to stress, and (particularly in older children and teenagers) eating disorders and addictions.

I believe that many of these problems are preventable, and it's never too late to repair your relationship with your child. (See Chapters

4 and 5 for more information.) In the United States we seem to prefer to wait for a problem to manifest itself before we address it, but a preventive approach is almost always easier, less expensive, and more effective. Notice I didn't say less painful. Prevention requires thought, it requires reflection, it requires effort, and it requires sacrifice, which requires some pain. Yet in my opinion, prevention is far superior to addressing problems after they have occurred. Reflection can be painful because it requires you to remember the past and feel emotions you may have tucked away for safekeeping. But, as I tell my patients, I find the avoidance of conflict and pain almost always causes more pain eventually.

Subtler forms of emotional abuse and neglect, such as chronic absence and misattunement, are as toxic to children as more extreme forms. When painful feelings are buried or ignored, they have consequences for emotional security, personality development, and resilience to stress throughout a person's life. Sometimes when I press my patients to recall painful childhood experiences, they argue that they never really had any. "I had enough food, a nice home, my parents gave me lots of stuff and sent me to good schools. So what do I have to complain about?" Of course, these things are wonderful (and in the case of enough food, essential). But they are not replacements for a lack of emotional connection, affection, and security, or a child's feeling that he is not interesting or important because that is how he sees himself in his mother's eyes, which is the most common root cause of emotional disturbance, mental illness, and social disorders.

For the past thirty years, researchers have been studying mothers and children across different cultures, and their findings have confirmed what I and my fellow psychoanalysts and therapists have seen in our practices: that infants and toddlers who have the constant and consistent presence of an attentive and sensitive mother are more likely to be emotionally and psychologically healthy children and adolescents.

Note that I say "more likely." A mother's physical or emotional absence doesn't condemn a child to a lifetime of social or emotional problems, but it does make it more likely that these problems will occur. There are always children who will weather the storms of frustration or separation more easily. However, many more children than previously thought are born genetically sensitive to stressors, including a mother's absence, maternal depression, or a lack of attention. The most important thing to remember about sensitive babies is that they are more common than you might realize. It's the nurturing environment that changes the potential outcome for these children's mental health.

Anxiety: Attentional Difficulties

Humans have not always been at the top of the food chain. We are all born with certain fears: fear of predators, fear of startling noises, fear of strange situations and strangers—it is these fears that have helped keep humans as a species alive.

When we are afraid, our limbic system (a set of brain structures that helps to regulate emotions that are related to survival) goes into high gear: the amygdala, a small, almond-shaped part of our brain, goes on alert and signals the hypothalamus, a section of the brain that produces many of the hormones that regulate our body functions, to signal the pituitary gland, which in turn signals the adrenal glands to release hormones like adrenaline (epinephrine) and cortisol into the bloodstream. This is called the HPA (hypothalamus-pituitary-adrenal) axis.

Adrenaline and cortisol are the fight-or-flight hormones. Adrenaline causes the heart to beat faster, pushing blood to the muscles, heart, and vital organs. Pulse rate and blood pressure rise and the rate of breathing increases to take in more oxygen, which is sent to the brain, increasing alertness. Cortisol triggers the release of blood sugar (glucose) and fats from temporary storage sites, and these nutrients flood into the bloodstream, supplying energy to all parts of the body. Cortisol also helps shut off the stress response after the threat is gone. The amygdala is responsible for stimulating the production of dopamine, which can increase focus and the cognitive processes necessary to cope with stress.[2] All this prepares us to face an enemy or run fast enough to escape, if necessary. When the threat is over, hormone levels, heart rate, and breathing return to normal. Tracy Bale said, "Stress response is perfectly normal. It's your body's way of making sure that whenever you need to respond to hunger, noise, or whatever the stressor is, that you are responding appropriately. Just because cortisol level[s] go up when you're stressed, that's what they're supposed to do. It's not stress in the moment that's damaging, it's chronic stress over time."

One of the tests used to determine the stress that babies are under is the salivary cortisol test, which analyzes a drop of saliva. Megan Gunnar, et al., at the University of Minnesota, did a study showing that babies who are separated from their mothers in the Strange Situation Experiment (described on page 60) show higher levels of cortisol in their saliva.[3]

A baby expects to be nurtured and protected by her mother; Mom is her buffer against an often-overwhelming world. Regina Sullivan, a neurobiology researcher and professor of child and adolescent psychiatry at New York University Langone Medical Center, studies fear in animals. Her research has shown that mothers, through their physical and emotional presence, help regulate the fear response in their offspring by reducing processing in the brain's fear center (the amygdala), which decreases the production of adrenaline, cortisol, and dopamine. Research suggests that without that physical and emotional presence, a baby who frequently feels threatened or afraid will become hypervigilant and will not see the world as a safe place.[4]

Brain scans of toddlers who have been deprived of emotional nurturing and who were physically neglected by their parents or caregivers (like those children who spent extended time in a Romanian orphanage or some foster care situations) reveal disproportionately large and active limbic systems.[5] For these children, it is as if the amygdala were stuck in the on position, with the hippocampus failing to shut down the production of the fight-or-flight hormones (like cortisol). As a result, those hormones remain in the body, and the child is always anxious and on the defensive, even when there's nothing to be afraid of; this is like a soldier with PTSD. Thus it is difficult for these toddlers to focus for long on any one activity, and even staying in one place can feel frightening.

Hypervigilance is at the core of many attention issues in children; it impacts their ability to learn, to relate to others socially, and to comfort themselves. According to the Child Mind Institute's Mental Health Report, hypervigilance or anxiety disorders have a median age of onset of six, which means that many children younger than six show signs of anxiety.[6] A chronically anxious child may be overly aggressive or very fearful and clingy. Some children become very demanding and difficult to soothe under any circumstances. As infants approach toddlerhood, this anxiety may express itself as difficulty paying attention, the inability to focus for long, or hyperactivity. Too much dopamine may also be responsible for problems with attention as well as learning and problem solving.

If a child's stress system is always activated, it may become blunted, or *hypo*vigilant. Dr. Nim Tottenham, of Columbia University, found that beginning when a baby is about one year of age you can see the changes that have been caused by too much stress in the limbic system of his brain, specifically the amygdala. After speaking to a number of researchers, I suspect that when a child is stressed, the amygdala activates and enlarges. A Stanford University study found that an enlarged amygdala correlates to increased anxiety in children (and adults).[7] When the stress is chronic, the amygdala works overtime, essentially poisoning itself with stress hormones and burning itself out. Studies have shown that adults suffering from PTSD have shrunken amygdalae.[8] It's like a lightbulb that gets too much current and blows out. In children, this manifests as dissociative behavior: They appear depressed or anxious and seem emotionally detached from what is going on around them.

One in ten children is diagnosed with ADHD in the United States.[9] These are only the diagnosed cases. Such children are often identified in preschool, which is when parents come to see me for guidance. The symptoms their children show are an inability to sit for long in the classroom; difficulty staying engaged in any one activity for long; the need to get up and move their bodies when they are in a social setting, often (but not always) accompanied by impulsive aggressive behavior like hitting or biting.

In the United States, ADD/ADHD is a diagnosis that is too frequently used to describe depression and anxiety in children. Other countries, like France, consider ADD and ADHD as psychosocial disorders and treat the conditions by focusing on the underlying cause with psychotherapy and family counseling, an approach with which I strongly agree.[10] This approach takes time and effort on the part of the parents. All too often, the response in the United States is to treat the symptoms with medication, rather than try to figure out why a child is struggling in this way.

Ritalin and Adderall are the two most frequently prescribed drugs for treating ADD/ADHD, and they are being prescribed to younger and younger children.[11] These drugs are central nervous system stimulants that work by increasing dopamine levels; we don't yet know what the long-term effects of changing the brain's chemical balance are on a child's developing body and mind. The best analogy I can use is when you drink a cup of coffee it energizes you, but when you drink too much it makes you feel sleepy and slows you down. Like the French, I see treating the child with play therapy and working with the parents as a better alternative to medication. Yes, there are some cases for which medication can be used in conjunction with psychotherapy for a limited time, while the parents work with their child to understand and address these behaviors, but I do not believe that medication should ever be used as the sole treatment for these disorders.

We are not born with the ability to sustain our focus; babies learn how to focus and increase their attention span from interacting with their mothers. This requires a mother to be interested in her child and what she is doing and to be able to focus her own attention on her baby without being constantly distracted. Showing an active interest, both verbally and nonverbally in your child—talking to your baby, singing, making faces, and playing peekaboo—are all simple forms of right brain to right brain interaction that have a profound effect on your child's emotional, cognitive, and physical development.

> Babies learn how to focus and increase their attention span from interacting with their mothers.

Of course, you can't play with your baby every minute; when an alert baby doesn't have his mother's attention, he will turn to objects or his own hand or foot to occupy him. Girls are better at waiting for their mother's attention than boys, who are more sensitive and will often become fractious or cry when their mothers are occupied. Boys' brains are also more susceptible to the effects of cortisol and anxiety, and a boy who is left to deal with his own distress or discomfort, unable to soothe himself, is more likely to be diagnosed with ADD/ADHD and behavioral problems than a girl will be. According to the Child

Mind Institute, there are twice as many boys (12.1 percent) as girls (5.5 percent) diagnosed with ADHD.[12]

Anxiety: Increased Aggression and Behavioral Problems

Aggression is one of the most common symptoms I see in toddlers. All children are born—to a greater or lesser degree—aggressive. It's a survival mechanism: When you are hungry, you cry; when you're not fed, you cry louder, and then you scream until someone comes. This is a healthy response, and if a baby's cries are quickly met by an emotionally responsive mother (or caregiver), who either feeds or comforts him, he stops crying. In a conversation with me, Judi Mesman, who has studied mother–child relationships around the world, noted: "Infants cry, but not as much in other cultures. Children are so close to their caregivers almost all of the time that there's really not so much of a need to cry, and when they do cry, their mother or caregiver reacts quickly. The term *colic babies* just doesn't exist."

Some babies are born with a more developed ability to demand that their needs be met; others have a harder time indicating what they need. Parents with a demanding or sensitive baby must begin by addressing that baby's needs as soon as possible, and over time they can help their infant learn to tolerate increasing amounts of frustration.

A baby who seems content to lie quietly without fussing or who does not demand attention may be perceived as "good" or "easy," but he's not always the healthiest baby. This baby's easy temperament may be a defensive reaction because his needs are not being met; often these babies exhibit failure to thrive or feeding issues. I think a demanding baby is actually easier to care for, because he lets you know that he needs something. Mothers must be more sensitive to a quiet, more passive baby so they do not miss his cues.

Aggression becomes a problem only when it interferes with a

child's functioning at home or in school. Without aggression, we cannot function in the world and develop a sense of self. Normal amounts of aggression drive children to learn, to reach for a desired object, to become mobile, and achieve competence in everyday skills. Sublimation is the process of channeling aggression in the right direction so it can become ambition, self-satisfaction, and self-confidence. This process requires a present mother who can help regulate a child's impulses and, without judgment or retaliation, set boundaries for his behavior.

When a baby cries because he's hungry or wants to be held, and you don't get there immediately, he gets angry with you, and that scares him. When a toddler gets angry at you because he can't go outside in the winter in his sandals, his anger scares him. When you meet your child's anger and frustration (whatever the reason) with empathy and calm and don't get upset or angry yourself (and that can be a challenge, I know), it helps your child feel less overwhelmed and transforms the anger into something less frightening. If you become impatient, or walk away without comforting your child, that feels to him like rejection or a punishment; he is likely to internalize his anger (rather than direct it at you), which can result in depression or anxiety.

From an evolutionary or neurobiological perspective, intense or defensive aggression in children is a response to danger or fear. When a baby is not comforted when she is distressed for too long or is understimulated because she isn't cuddled or played with for too long, she begins to feel fearful. If she learns that she cannot rely on a predictable, soothing, loving mother, that fear often turns to aggression, or if the baby internalizes her anger and fear, it becomes depression. Let me be clear that I'm not talking about the couple of times you were in the shower when your baby woke up and cried and you couldn't get to her right away. Babies learn to cope with that kind of acute but transitory fear, especially if they are soothed quickly.

Defensive aggression is a response to a chronic perception of danger that triggers feelings of loss and rejection because a child has not had his fundamental needs for love, nurturing, and security met. If a child feels safe, then there's no need for him to try to protect himself. Think of your child as a pitcher and you as the catcher. If your child throws a wild pitch, you catch it so it doesn't hurt you or another person. Your child learns to trust that you will help him not to hurt himself or someone else, and eventually, usually around the age of two, he will internalize that sense of control. If there is no one there to catch the pitch or you react with an aggressive throw in retaliation, your child feels abandoned, guilty, and frightened of his own anger.

This increased aggression often manifests in toddlers as the inability to tolerate frustration. It may take the form of hitting, biting, pushing, or other impulsive responses, like knocking down the Lego construction of another child at school, getting up during circle or quiet time, or verbally assaulting other children or adults. A child may ignore or deliberately flout rules set by parents or teachers. Toddler boys may experience a surge of testosterone, which can increase their aggressive and/or impulsive behavior; this does not necessarily indicate that there's a larger problem. As we have pushed our children to become more autonomous and begin preschool younger, what some people call "boy energy" has been pathologized.

Children used to start preschool at four; until then they stayed with their mother, who acted as their constant emotional regulator, especially for aggression. Today many programs take children as young as eighteen months; that's a big difference in terms of a child's emotional and physical development as well as his impulse control and ability to toilet train. Changes in routine and environment, even small changes, can also trigger what we call regressive behavior—a child who's been successfully toilet trained begins to wet his pants, or one who has been relatively even tempered hits or bites a classmate. It's unrealistic to expect a two-and-a-half-year-old—especially a boy—to be able to sit quietly or contain his boundless physical energy in circle time. What some people see as misbehavior, "acting out," or symptoms of ADD or ADHD I see as a normal, if unfortunate, reaction to being separated from his mother before a child is developmentally ready.

Some people think that hitting and biting are normal (but not acceptable) toddler behavior. When it happens outside the home, it's not. That kind of physical aggression is a sign of anxiety and depression, and a sign that the child needs help. The normal pattern of behavior is that kids act out at home, where they feel safe, and behave at school, daycare, or around strangers. Almost every parent I know has been surprised by a teacher, or parent of a child's friend, who praised their child's behavior in the classroom or on a playdate.

Children model their parents' behavior. Mothers and fathers who can control their own anger and frustration (which is sometimes difficult when you're dealing with a stubborn toddler, I know!) are teaching their children to tolerate frustration and regulate their aggression.

> Children model their parents' behavior.

In working with children who have anger issues, I have found that often the mothers and fathers have issues similar to the child's. I helped a family because the school was concerned the child was very bossy and aggressive with his peers, who thus no longer wanted to play with him. In treating the mother, I discovered she was also extremely controlling at home, literally telling her son what and how to build with his blocks. A mother who struggles to regulate her own aggressive impulses may become depressed or angry when she has to deal with her baby's or toddler's needs. Afraid that she won't be able to handle her own feelings, she may believe that by leaving her baby in the care of others she's doing what's best for her and her child. However, if she runs from her feelings rather than explores their source, she may never get the help she needs, and both child and mother suffer.

The original meaning of the word *discipline* was "to teach by example," not to punish or judge a child. Mothers provide the external guide to appropriate behavior and emotional control for a child; eventually the child internalizes these lessons as self-control and self-discipline. Often when mothers are not physically present enough or are depressed or excessively aggressive themselves, their child may have difficulty internalizing self-control. Discipline also requires that a mother be self-aware about her own emotions, so she can help her child regulate his emotions.

Studies from the 1980s through 2015[13] have shown that children in daycare express more aggression by school age than children cared for by their mothers or with a single surrogate caregiver. Babies thrive in an intimate relationship with a primary caregiver, preferably their mother; they are overwhelmed by interacting with many caregivers who are tending too many children to focus on the emotional needs of any individual child. (For more about why a single caregiver or relative is a better childcare option when a mother must work outside the home, see Chapter 6.)

Both boys and girls may show aggressive symptoms in response to neglect or to feeling abandoned by their mothers. Boys are usually more aggressive than girls in response to these feelings because they have more testosterone. But boys are often also more sensitive than girls; given the same kind of emotional environment, a boy may have a stronger and more intense response to neglect or a stressor, such as maternal depression, anxiety, or intrusiveness (the inability to allow a child to become frustrated or to explore on his own and, later, overinvolvement or helicopter parenting). There is also evidence that, in general, boys develop more autistic-like symptoms than girls; this is related to their sensitivity to environmental stress. Girls tend to have

term memory. The teachers said he would probably have ADHD and learning issues."

What was more important, Simone believed, is that she was able to take a leave of absence from her job so she "could dedicate time to [Alec] and help him to feel emotionally secure." With the help of tutors and specialists, as well as his mother's time and attention, Alec's relationship with his mother strengthened, his anxiety lessened, and his social skills improved.

When her second child, Leo, was born, Simone took a longer maternity leave and went back to work part-time. "I can see the difference in my two sons," she told me, "because of the time I took to make my second son feel secure and to be there for him emotionally. My only regret is that I didn't take more time after Alec was born and went back to work full-time. I only wish I had known how important it is to be there for your children earlier."

Lack of Resilience to Stress

The mechanism for stress resilience is found in the right side and limbic system of the brain. How resilient a baby is and the adult she will become depend on her secure attachment, connection, and interaction with her mother or primary caregiver. If a mother is physically present but is emotionally unable to connect with her child, her emotional absence is as painful as if she were not there at all. Many of my adult patients have described the terrible emptiness of having a mother who ignored or misinterpreted their needs.

When a baby is securely attached to her mother and her mother is present to help moderate the baby's emotions, the limbic system continues to provide the baby with the same regulatory function as her mother, even when the mother is absent for short periods of time. Babies internalize the stress-buffering their mothers provide, and it becomes part of their protection in the future. However, when a mother is absent emotionally and/or physically, the limbic system does not develop enough to protect the baby from the emotional and physical effects of stress and fear.

Earlier I explained how anxiety is often the result of a reaction to fear. It is a baby's secure relationship with his mother that serves as a buffer against the fears babies inevitably feel. Cuddling and touch from a present mother are potent antidotes to stress. Remember Michael Meaney, whose research showed that mother rats that licked and groomed their young on a regular basis had offspring that showed reduced levels of stress hormones and were more resilient to stress? Meaney also found that there is a generational transmission of the ability to lick and groom; rats that were nurtured by their mothers also nurtured their own young; the young that were not licked and groomed did not.[19] The same is true for humans: When mothers cannot nurture their young because they are bored, disinterested, or distracted—or simply because they aren't there—it has the same generational impact on their babies.

Bowlby called the ability to cope with environmental stress "the internal scaffolding of the baby," and it is put in place and secured by the ability of a mother to soothe and comfort her baby in the early years.[20] Without this scaffolding, or when the scaffolding is not secured by the mother because of maternal absence or depression, the baby is at a higher risk for vulnerability to environmental stressors. The inability to regulate stress or lack of resilience to stress may in fact be responsible for many mental disorders, including depression, anxiety, and addictions as well as physical illnesses such as heart disease, diabetes, cancer, and even obesity. Steve Cole of UCLA has explored how environmental stressors increase the risk of a person's chance of becoming ill, particularly in individuals who have been deprived of essential nurturing.[21]

Disorders of the Self in Adolescents and Adults

So far I have focused on what may happen to young children when their mothers are less present emotionally and physically. However, it's equally important to understand the long-term impact of this absence on adolescents and adults.

There has been a dramatic increase among adolescents in alcoholism and drug addiction, eating disorders, depression, and anxiety. Statistics published by the National Institute of Mental Health show that 8 percent of adolescents between the ages of thirteen and eighteen currently have an anxiety disorder, and 25.1 percent of adolescents will experience a lifelong anxiety disorder.[22] The Renfrew Center for Eating Disorders estimated that 25 percent of teenage girls and college students have some form of a bingeing and purging eating disorder.[23] The National Center on Addiction and Substance Abuse called adolescent substance abuse epidemic: 46 percent of high school students use addictive substances, including cigarettes, alcohol, and drugs, and 12 percent meet the clinical criteria for addiction.[24] These conditions are disorders of the self, and when someone suffers from one of them, it means they have not internalized a secure sense of self, or who they are. Instead of internalizing a comforting and loving mother, there is a critical voice, or the hollowness from feeling unloved, unseen, and unrecognized.

A child's sense of self develops slowly and in response to the intimate interaction and communication between mother and baby. When a child feels that her mother finds her interesting and understands how she is feeling much of the time, she feels valued and lovable; this forms the basis of a secure sense of self.

A person's ability to withstand stress and regulate intense emotions as a young adult largely depends on this maternal support. All children have two mothers. First is their real, or external, mother who may be loving, sensitive, and present or detached, insensitive, and absent. This mother can do a great deal of good and/or damage, but a child has no control over who his mother is and whether she meets his needs. However, there is another mother, the internal mother, who is inside of every child (and in all of us). The internal mother is a reflection—and often an exaggeration—of the positive and negative qualities of the real mother. If a child had a present mother, she is the voice in his head that comforts and nurtures him when he is in distress and bolsters his confidence and self-esteem. If a child had an absent or critical mother, that internal conversation may be very different: The internal mother may be critical of the child's feelings and behavior and may even be impossible to find when he needs her for support and reassurance.

A child whose mother is unavailable emotionally and physically will often develop an emotional shell, like a hard candy coating over a soft and vulnerable interior. This protective defense allows a child to function but not function well, and whenever he feels in distress his soft and vulnerable center cannot provide him with a solid sense of security. Often these children (and later as adults) have an inflated and unsubstantiated sense of their abilities, power, and authority, which collapses when they're under pressure or faced with adversity or setbacks.

Again, it is important to reiterate that whether someone develops depression, anxiety, or disorders of the self depends not only on the foundation of a child's security but also on the experiences and relationships that occur throughout his life. Think of infancy and toddlerhood as having a wormhole to adolescence, where all the emotional and psychological issues that were unresolved in toddlerhood get replayed, on a more unforgiving stage. If a child had a present and sensitive mother, then he has a greater chance of weathering the turbulence of adolescence when hormonal changes, identity struggles, and social difficulties strain already weak defenses. However, if a child had a rough beginning because his mother was absent emotionally and/or physically and there was no one to help regulate his emotions, there is a good chance the coping behaviors that might have served him well in early childhood, whether increased aggression or withdrawal, can create problems with grave consequences in adolescence. Michael Numan and Tom Insel studied the biology of parental behavior.[25] They described the effects of a lack of emotional sustenance, which impacts the reward system in a child's brain and may predispose a child to later addictive behavior. For many of such teens, the bottom drops out, and they have breakdowns that take the form of depression, anxiety, eating disorders, and addictions of all kinds, including drugs, alcohol, and sexual promiscuity.[26]

The treatment for disorders of the self—including addictions—is reflective psychotherapy. In this situation, the therapist interacts right brain to right brain with the patient, just as a sensitive mother interacts with her baby, essentially trying to jump-start the development of the right social emotional brain, which may have been interrupted, and create a supportive, loving internal mother. (In contrast, cognitive behavioral therapy addresses specific behaviors, not the cause, and appeals to the left side of the brain.)

While many young adults with disorders of the self can often be helped through reflective psychotherapy, it is much harder to treat than if such conditions are identified earlier in childhood. Intervention with parent guidance when children are beginning to show signs they are in pain is important; the sooner we intervene, the easier it is to repair the damage that is causing a child's behavior and symptoms.

CHAPTER 8

When Mothers Turn Away

Postpartum Depression and the Legacy of Absence

In his book *Identity and the Life Cycle*, psychoanalyst and architect of the theory of psychosocial stages Erik Erikson offers a model of psychological development in which having children of one's own is a milestone.[1] What Erikson doesn't say is that having children before you have resolved conflicted or ambivalent feelings about being a nurturing mother can result in depression, anxiety, and a desire to abdicate or avoid your maternal role.

In almost all cultures, marrying and having children has been an important part of a woman's identity. In most cultures, including our own, it is still expected that at some point in her life most women will get married and have children. Becoming a mother is not an obligation, and it is not a necessary step to becoming an adult; the question we should be asking is whether every woman should, in fact, take this path. You can be a mature and emotionally healthy woman and decide that marriage or a long-term committed relationship or motherhood is not part of your life plan, especially if you have creative or meaningful work (paid or unpaid).

Women who plan to have children should think carefully about the many issues they will face. How do they define their core values? Do they believe that family comes first or that work and status will take priority in their lives? Are they having children because they want to nurture a child or because it's expected of them? Do they need to work to support their family or would it make more financial sense to stay home with their child? If they stay home, will they be comfortable with the loss of status and loss of income? If they go back to work, can they be clear about their own boundaries regarding when and how much they will work? Can they be clear with their employers about what those boundaries are, and are they prepared to enforce them, and deal with any possible consequences to their careers? Do their spouses or partners share their values and priorities and support their decision, whatever the decision may be?

Motherhood should be a choice, and that choice requires recognizing the sacrifices involved in being a mother and working through conflicts about mothering before having a child. We take it for granted that when a woman has a child or wants to have a child that she has come to terms with all of her feelings about being a mother, but all too often this is not true. We take for granted that our desire to be a mother is based on our ability to be a mother, but it is important to understand where desire comes from. Sigmund Freud and his followers in the psychoanalytic movement believe that we have conscious wishes that are easily accessible; unconscious wishes and fears that can be reached through dreams, artistic expression, free association, and psychotherapy; and subconscious wishes. Subconscious wishes live close to the surface of our consciousness; they can be confusing and often disturbing when we are aware of them, particularly if they conflict with our conscious desires.[2]

A woman may have a strong conscious desire to *have* a baby, but this is not mutually exclusive of having conflicting feelings about mothering or *caring* for a baby. It is important to remember that the desire to have a baby is driven, in part, by biology (and reinforced by culture). The desire to *care for* or nurture a totally dependent baby requires a woman to connect with a positive experience of being nurtured by her own mother. It's common for a woman to have the fantasy that her child will satisfy her own unmet needs for love and attention, particularly if she had a conflicted or turbulent relationship with her own mother. When a woman idealizes the experience of motherhood before she has experienced it, particularly if she has had a difficult relationship with her own mother, she may be setting herself up for disappointment. For many vulnerable women, this can be a catalyst for postpartum depression and can trigger her rejection of mothering. Childbirth is painful; the aftermath of childbirth is uncomfortable and messy; breastfeeding is often frustrating until you get the hang of it. Interrupted sleep is the norm for the first two years of your child's life, but most intensely for the first few months after your child is born. There's never (or very rarely) a day off. Caring for a baby is damn hard work.

What was your own experience of your mother? Did you feel she was emotionally and physically available to you? Did you feel she was interested in you and found you interesting? Or was she bored and eager to get away from you? Did she comfort you when you were distressed? Did you feel accepted or rejected? These are critical questions to ask yourself before you have children.

When we have a positive experience with our mother we are more likely to know how to mother our own babies. Mothering is generational. The drive to reproduce is instinctual, and the ability to nurture is in our DNA as women, but it must be turned on by the environment. If a very young child's environment—which is their mother— impacts their mental health, then it doesn't matter whether that mother lives in a $2-million apartment on Park Avenue, in a suburban colonial outside of Chicago, in a mobile home in Alabama, or in public housing in Detroit if she is emotionally and physically present. Studies by Dr. Michael Meaney and by Dr. Tom Insel, neuroscientist and former director of the National Institute of Mental Health, have shown that maternal behavior is passed from generation to generation. Insel called this "maternal memory."[3] However, if a mother animal does not nurture her young, the ability to nurture is not passed down to the next generation.[4] In Harry Harlow's experiments with rhesus monkeys, babies who were taken away from their mothers immediately after they were born did not know how to mother when they in turn gave birth.[5]

If our own mothers were not present enough physically or emotionally, then we likely did not learn how to be present with our own babies. Although not all mothers who are absent are depressed, depression is a very common cause of emotional absence. Research has shown us that genetics and the environment combine to increase the rates of mental illness in children of mothers with depression. Marian Radke-Yarrow studied mothers suffering from depression and how they affected their children. Her findings were published by the National Institute of Mental Health.[6] The women Radke-Yarrow studied often felt sad; had low self-esteem, disturbed sleep or appetite, and mood swings; and had lost interest in activities they had previously enjoyed. They felt they were "bad" mothers; they did not enjoy playing with their children, often misread or ignored their children's cues and needs, and were often angry and impatient, emotionally withholding, or absent.

The study found that between the ages of eighteen months and three and a half years old, a third of the children of mothers suffering from depression showed some signs of normal separation anxiety (signs of mild anxiety when their mothers left them), but a third of them expressed frequent, intense, and extreme separation anxiety, and the remaining third showed oppositional-defiant aggressive behavior (being uncooperative, hostile, and disruptive, beyond the usual behavior for a child's age). That is, two-thirds of the children of depressed mothers had behavior issues and anxiety as opposed to 16.7 percent overall of children of well mothers. In addition, 38 percent of the children of depressed mothers were insecurely attached and showed signs of depression themselves. By the time the children of depressed mothers were five to seven years old, 64.3 percent had social or emotional problems, and when they reached adolescence, the rate was 57.7 percent.[7]

In my practice, over the past ten years there has been an increase in mothers who express very ambivalent feelings about mothering. This is in part an expression of a new honesty about what some women experience as the realities of motherhood, which is supported and encouraged by blogs and other social media. This is a good thing for mothers who may not have had an outlet to express such feelings, but it's not an indication that all mothers feel this way. More concerning, it's a sign that these women are dealing with feelings of hurt, rejection, and sadness about their own early childhood experiences. According to a 1992 study by Les Whitbeck and coworkers, adults who recalled being rejected by their parents were more likely to be depressed and have difficulty relating to their own children.[8] These women may not be getting the help they need to deal with these wounds. What are the costs to their children of having mothers who are angry or resentful much of the time?

In my profession we refer to "neurotic repetition," which means people repeat what was done to them, often in an effort to resolve painful feelings. (The definition of the word *neurotic* is "to be in conflict.") Whether she has one or five children, a mother will often find herself interacting with her own infant in the same manner as her mother did with her. The problem with this is that unless a mother has been able to resolve the ambivalent feelings she has about her own mother, it is likely that her behavior will not change. The painful recognition that this is happening in spite of their conscious desire to act differently often makes women want to run away from their role as mothers rather than face the ambivalence.

The human psyche is amazingly adaptable until it isn't. When we are hurt or have painful or traumatic experiences, our mind protects itself from the pain by utilizing defenses (different for each person) that help us not just to survive the trauma but to function in spite of it. These defenses range from denying that we feel the pain at all to redefining the experience(s) as good (character building, for example) rather than bad (my mother didn't comfort me when I broke my arm). We may put the memories in the deepest lockbox of our unconscious or we may feel angry or we may feel like we're always being persecuted and never know why.

> The human psyche is amazingly adaptable until it isn't.

We understand and accept the damage that extreme neglect does to children. In his book *Romania's Abandoned Children*, Charles Nelson detailed how these children, whose emotional needs were never met, who were allowed to cry, and who were never picked up or cuddled, have been severely impacted emotionally and cannot function socially.[9] But there is a more subtle and nuanced form of emotional neglect, and I see its effects on both parents and children in my practice all the time.

Infants or very young children may have all their physical needs met, but if they do not have their emotional needs *consistently* met—

that is, if they cannot rely on their mother to respond when they need her (for whatever reason)—they develop what psychologists call defensive, or stress-inoculated, independence as a survival mechanism. Instead of reaching for their mothers when they return from work or the day away, these children push their mothers away and refuse to be hugged or interact. When this type of independence is shown by children three and under, parents often misinterpret it as a positive thing, but it's actually a sign of a problem with attachment. As these independent children get older, they are more likely to experience anxiety and depression but don't connect it to their own early experiences and the pain of being rejected or ignored. They often have relationship difficulties throughout life because they lack the ability to attach to others deeply and to feel deeply.

Children of this kind of emotional neglect often repeat this pattern with their own children. When I work with a patient, what we often discover is that her difficulty with her children has everything to do with her confusing feelings about her own experience of her mother. When a mother tells me "I'm so bored with my infant," or "I'm just overwhelmed and can't wait to get away from my baby," what I hear behind these statements is a profound and painful feeling that her own mother found her boring and rejected her needs.

Ann, twenty-eight, was an assistant in the fashion industry. She came to see me because her eighteen-month-old son, Jason, was rejecting her when she returned home from work in the evening. Ann breastfed Jason; in fact, she let the baby nurse constantly, because, she told me, she was afraid that when she put him down she wouldn't want to pick him up again. She stopped nursing when she returned to work when Jason was three months old.

Ann was eager to get back to her job, and often worked late.

Her husband had a more flexible schedule, so he dropped Jason off at daycare and picked him up at the end of the day. Because Ann often worked so late, he took care of their son in the evening until Ann arrived, often after the baby was asleep.

Ann told me that she felt sad and alone and insecure about not being able to mother, which are warning signs for post-partum depression. As soon as Ann came home from the hospital, she felt out of sorts, but she didn't understand *why* she was feeling so blue. She was jealous of Jason's attachment to her husband. She felt anxious around her son when she spent too much time with him, but when Jason rejected her she felt it like a sword through her heart.

Ann's mother had left her alone much of the time when she was a younger, and while Ann's mother ran the household efficiently ("We never ran out of milk or detergent," Ann told me), she wasn't affectionate, or sympathetic when Ann was sad after her turtle died, or upset when she had a fight with a friend. In addition, she didn't enjoy spending time with her grandson.

Because Ann grew up feeling she could not depend on her mother for comfort, she was uncomfortable with her own baby's need for her and was unconsciously repeating with her son the relationship her mother had with her. She was able to recognize that her sadness and anger toward her own mother was fueling her ambivalence toward caring for Jason.

Ann made an effort to get home from work earlier so she could spend more time with Jason in the evening and put him to bed. Though she continued to struggle with her son's need for her, Ann found she felt closer to Jason. Her son stopped pushing his mother away, and the closeness of their early days of breastfeeding returned.

For a woman, having a baby can open the floodgates of repressed or hidden emotions. That is often when mothers have a breakdown, as in postpartum depression, or come to me with feelings of depression or anxiety that may be delayed postpartum depression responses. Repression is a great thing if it holds, but like the proverbial can of worms, when the defenses that a person has used her whole life break down, all of the sadness and loss that is connected to feeling your mother was not there enough when you were little starts leaking out of the lockbox of the unconscious. Most people think that postpartum depression is caused by hormonal changes, but in many cases it is more complex, involving the absence of a good enough internal mother to support, validate, reassure, and soothe a new mother. A woman who suffers from the classic signs of depression, like Ann, may have had an emotionally absent mother, whereas a mother who is overly anxious may have had a more aggressive or intrusive mother. Think of hormones as the catalyst or key that opens the storeroom door full of painful feelings and memories.

Postpartum depression (PPD) impacts 10 to 15 percent of women who give birth.[10] It affects women across socioeconomic lines and is, in my opinion, one of the greatest barriers to healthy attachment and bonding with one's baby. PPD comes in many forms. It may be experienced as mild depression and anxiety on one end of the spectrum and can manifest as psychotic thoughts of killing one's baby and oneself on the other; and it can be many things in between. PPD most often takes the form of pervasive sadness, lethargy, the inability to take care of oneself or one's baby, feelings of hopelessness and helplessness, and mood swings. When PPD takes this form it's usually recognized by spouses, close family and friends, obstetricians, and pediatricians. But there are other, more subtle signs of PPD, which may be more difficult to identify but are equally damaging to mother and child.

The most common form of PPD I see comes in the form of mothers who can't take being with their babies for too long. Many women who have only had to care for themselves their entire lives may feel frustrated and overwhelmed when they realize that have to put their own needs on hold to care for a new baby twenty-four hours a day. They want to run away or go back to work, back to the life they had before. It's a kind of denial that their lives have changed forever. These women tell themselves they will be a better mother when the children are older and need them less. The problem? A baby cannot develop into an emotionally healthy, interdependent person without being intensely dependent first. To be a present mother, a woman must be able set aside her own needs and then gradually reclaim what is important to her as her child matures and needs her less.

We understand that PPD is more likely to occur in women who have a history of anxiety and/or mild depression, who may have suffered great stress or felt depressed feelings during pregnancy, and who are isolated with these feelings due to shame and embarrassment. Through this book, I hope to reach and educate young women before they have children to seek help so that when the time comes to make the decision to become a mother, it is made healthfully and wisely, with conflicts mostly resolved and eyes wide open. Although not every new mother has access to insight-oriented psychotherapy when they are raising children, they should seek help, particularly if they are showing signs or having symptoms of PPD. The purpose of insight-oriented therapy is to help people resolve internal conflicts and deal with painful feelings—between what they want and how they go about getting it, between feeling one way and acting another, between what they want to do and what they have to do. Insight-oriented therapy seeks to make mothers self-aware and understand how their past influences their present behavior, which is critical to change in a more sustainable way.

Julie, forty, came to see me because her three-and-a-half-year-old daughter, Sophie, had difficulty separating when she was dropped off at preschool. I'm not talking about the garden-variety separation response, but clinging to her mother, inconsolable sobbing, and screaming. Julie was often late for work because of the situation. Julie felt embarrassed by Sophie's reaction, guilty because her daughter was so unhappy, deeply sad about having to leave her daughter, and upset at herself for being angry at Sophie because she wouldn't behave.

Julie was a bookkeeper for a small company; her husband left for work before she did, and often came home later. Julie's company did not offer paid maternity leave; she had to return to work full-time when Sophie was six weeks old. Julie wished she could have spent more time at home with Sophie. She had struggled with her decision to put her into daycare and felt guilty and sad, especially when, at about nine months old, Sophie began to get upset when her mother left her. The staff at the daycare center told Julie that it took a long time, but Sophie would eventually calm down; however, she was uninterested in playing with the other children and rarely smiled.

Julie was raised in a single-parent household; she didn't remember a time when her mother, who worked at a local department store, didn't come home too exhausted to do anything but make dinner and collapse in front of the TV. She dismissed Julie's need for affection, and Julie learned to take care of herself, physically and emotionally. Julie's defensive independence made it difficult for her, when she became a mother, to accept her daughter's dependency.

Julie's sadness, unresolved guilt, anger, and resentment toward Sophie and her needs were symptoms of PPD, which were the result of unresolved issues from her own childhood.

By exploring her feelings of sadness and anger toward her own mother as well as her conflicted feelings about caring for Sophie, Julie was able to separate her sadness and defensiveness from her daughter's need of her. She became more reflective about Sophie's emotional needs and worked on her responses to Sophie in an empathic manner. This helped Julie learn how to look *toward* Sophie in her sadness rather than away, as she had previously done because it was too painful.

Once we explored Julie's fears about losing her job and about Sophie's dependency on her, Julie was able to make changes with her work situation that allowed her to be more present for Sophie. She spent more time with Sophie, particularly in the morning when she was transitioning to school, and her increased awareness of Sophie's fears, sadness, and need of her helped Julie be more emotionally present when she was with her daughter, making the separation easier for both of them. Not only did Julie benefit from reflecting on her own feelings and fears, but she also benefited from being able to think about her daughter's feelings. Once she was given permission, in a sense, to enjoy being with her daughter, things changed rather dramatically for the mother–daughter pair.

Another powerful example of how PPD manifests itself is the story of Joanna, fifty-two, who ran a successful public relations company. Her son, George, was born when she was thirty; Joanna said that he "came into the world kicking and screaming. He had colic for what felt like six years. He was very wound up and hard to soothe as an infant."

While Joanna was rising in the ranks of her company, she was also feeling incredibly unsuccessful at mothering. "I always thought that I could just take care of everything, and suddenly this one little thing is as overwhelming as everyone tells you. I am not someone who covers up my feelings, and people were extremely uncomfortable when I would talk about the challenges. I remember telling people I work with how I didn't really like my baby very much, and how I was so happy to go back to work so I didn't have to deal with this little person who couldn't connect with me." Joanna's anger toward her son and her resentment of being needed make up another example of PPD. Joanna didn't realize she was suffering from PPD or that it was connected to her painful childhood.

"There were symptoms like temper tantrums," Joanna recalled. "We couldn't calm George down and would actually have to remove ourselves from wherever he had a meltdown. George was very smart but had trouble regulating his emotions. When he went for interviews for schools when he was four, he drew exploding black volcanoes—and he didn't get into any school. He became very angry and had difficulty having close relationships with his peers. My husband encouraged therapy for him and it helped; he was able to manage himself and his emotions more effectively as a result."

Joanna came to recognize how her own relationship with her mother affected her. Her sister was so ill that she could not be cared for at home, and when her mother visited her she would never touch her: "I felt that I was the replacement for the child she had before me. My mother had an explosive temper and was literally depressed; she was never connected to her own mother. My mother was a very demanding person; she could be loving, but could be very cruel," she recounted. "When George was born, I was reliving my mother's situation with my sister, who she rejected when she was born, and I didn't realize it. I think it was my way of getting close to her.

One way my mother valued me was through my professional success; she used to say, 'I never thought that you would ever make something of yourself.'"

Joanna saw that George, then in his twenties, had trouble with relationships and self-esteem. He was a sweet and loving young man who was afraid of attaching. Joanna realized that she was part of the problem and still struggled with this issue in therapy. "In my family you just sucked it up and didn't go to therapy. I wish I had done it earlier; I wish I had asked for help." Joanna was a brave woman who was on the road to recovery, and so was her son.

Pediatricians, nurses, and nurse practitioners are the first line of defense against postpartum depression because they see mothers and newborns together on a regular basis. Unfortunately, because most medical professionals are concerned primarily with physical and behavioral issues, they may miss the signs that a mother is in distress. Or a woman may be so ashamed and embarrassed by her feelings that she doesn't want to discuss them. Even if a pediatrician is aware that the mother is suffering from postpartum depression, or is having trouble adjusting to her new role, many will refer a mother to a psychiatrist or doctor who will prescribe medication, rather than a psychotherapist for talk therapy.

Great Britain has an impressive health visitors program—every mother, no matter what her socioeconomic status, receives a health visitor at home almost immediately after the birth of her child and for the next four and a half years. The health visitor, who is a qualified registered nurse or midwife with additional training in maternal and child health and postpartum care, calls on the family within the first fourteen days after the birth of the child. She is there to teach and reinforce breastfeeding, to promote sensitive parenting, to educate parents on child development, to assess maternal mental health, and to assess the attachment of the baby and mother. The health visitor's involvement may prevent and resolve many issues before or as they are occurring; she can refer the mother to a talk therapist for help if necessary.[11]

At one time, most new mothers had many women around them before, during, and after birth. Mothers, aunts, sisters, cousins, grandmothers, and even neighbors shared stories of their own birth experiences, and made nourishing meals so that new mothers could recover their strength after labor. They took care of the house and the cooking so the mother could get to know her new baby. They taught new mothers that breastfeeding takes time and explained how to do so comfortably. They alleviated their concerns and cared for their babies so that they could get some much-needed sleep.

In our society, we have lost this circle of love among women, which leaves mothers isolated, confused, and alone at a time when they need care and support the most. Family often lives far away. A woman's mother (or mother-in-law) may come for a week or a few days or not at all. Sometimes she's not welcome. She may have different ideas of how to care for a newborn or disagree with the mother's decision on how to feed the baby, whether it's breast or bottle. A grandmother may feel she's done with nurturing, thank you very much, or she may be too tired, ill, or frail. She may not have resolved her own conflicts about mothering. A grandmother may not see herself in a nurturing role or may believe that mothering is less valuable than other pursuits.

> Carol, whose two children were teenagers, found it hard to be home with her first baby and returned to work full-time before her son was six months old because she had little support from her own mother and did not have a community

of women to lean on. "I found staying home with kids to be challenging. I was not adept at creating networks of mothers, which I think a lot of women who are used to being home do." Carol's father passed away when she was pregnant, and her mother died three months after her first child was born. Her husband's family and her siblings lived far away. "I was isolated and I was lonely. I found it really boring to get up and take a walk to the park or sit at home when my son napped. Just the relentless routine of caring for a baby without having adult companionship I found very trying. Maybe had I given it more time I would have made more of a community. I was losing my identity as a working person; being someone who didn't work scared me."

Carol described the difficulty her own mother had mothering: "My mother fed us and took care of the basics, but I don't remember her playing with us; she would take us to the beach and go off herself and swim for two hours. She told me that she was bored with being a mother. I think she was depressed. She wasn't terribly introspective on an emotional level, so I don't think she had regrets."

Carol felt like she tried to compensate for her own mother's emotional detachment by being affectionate with her own children, but even though she consciously made an effort, she still had the emotional standoffishness she learned from her mother. "I feel like I taught my kids to be very independent quickly and now sometimes they go off without looking back and don't even call at all; they don't seem to need contact with me."

Carol regretted that she imposed so much structure instead of being with her children. She said sadly, "I couldn't relax and enjoy mothering, I didn't spend much time with them on a daily basis. I wish I hadn't been so tired from work that I just wanted them to go to bed."

Like many mothers, Carol made the assumption that she would spend as much time and energy working outside the home after she had children as she had before. "I never really sat down and thought about it. It's a big decision and it shouldn't be made by default. I wish I had gotten in touch with myself and what my own needs were, what my own history was, and what kind of parent I wanted to be in order to make a wiser decision."

If you are thinking about having a baby or trying to get pregnant, this is the time to explore your feelings: positive, negative, and ambivalent.

If you are already pregnant, how do you feel about becoming a mother? Happy and excited? A little anxious about the demands and responsibilities? Or are you sad and maybe even a little depressed at the loss of your old life?

Getting pregnant in response to social or family pressure, because your spouse or partner wants you to, or because you want someone to love you the way you were never loved is not the healthiest reason to have a baby. And if your expectation is that as a mother you will be blissful all the time and always in harmony with your baby's needs, you are setting yourself up for a great disappointment.

Women often play down or deny the importance of their negative or ambivalent feelings when they think about having a baby, hoping that after the baby arrives all will be resolved. Quite the opposite is usually the case, however, because when the baby is born many of these complicated feelings tend to surface with a vengeance. It is far better to speak to a therapist or counselor *before* you become pregnant or have a baby to resolve many of these feelings and concerns; however, as we see from Joanna's story, it is never too late seek help and repair the relationship with your child. Seeking help or reflecting on these issues at *any* age can improve the mother–child relationship and also make way for the grandmother–grandchild relationship to come.

New Mothers Need Support

As the African proverb goes, "It takes a village to raise a child," but more important, it takes a village to care for a new mother. Build your support system before your baby is born: your spouse or partner, family, friends, doctor, pediatrician, a doula and/or surrogate caregiver(s). Often family who come to help a new mother leave after two weeks—just when your baby is waking up from his birth experience and is becoming active and demanding! In many cultures family and friends care for a new mother during the first month to six weeks after she gives birth; this is not considered a luxury but a necessity.

> It takes a village to care for a new mother.

When everyone leaves the party is when you feel most alone. It can be helpful for new mothers to join a support group, maternal yoga class, or birthing class where you can share your feelings with other mothers. Remember that mothers throughout history never went through pregnancy or raised children alone. It is critical to not be isolated when you are pregnant or raising children.

If you are feeling stressed or overwhelmed, before or during your pregnancy or after your baby is born, it is important that you share your feelings with your spouse and those closest to you. Many women feel ashamed of feeling ambivalent about having or caring for a baby; if you're not comfortable speaking to your partner, family, or friends, speak to your doctor. Open communication and expression of feelings are critical for mental health and well-being, particularly in mother-hood.

If you know you are prone to push away or deny painful feelings, resist the urge to push away or suppress your feelings of ambivalence or conflict when thinking about being a mother. It is easier to treat a woman while she is pregnant than after she gives birth; the earlier the intervention the better, though you can seek help at any time during your mothering arc, with great benefits to you and your child.

Babies are fascinating to observe and interact with, and their development is astonishingly and beautifully subtle while being dramatic at the same time. Being with a baby is like appreciating a piece of art that you didn't see completely at first, but after a second and third look you are enthralled. We are so accustomed to fast-moving and overstimulating sensory overload activities that we have lost the ability to appreciate and recognize the excitement in the way a baby is mesmerized by her tiny hand or the way she signals that she is hungry by rooting with her tongue. For every subtle gesture a baby makes, her brain cells are multiplying by the thousands. Baby watching is a very exciting experience, but even the most exciting experience has boring moments. If a mother returns to work too quickly or turns away from her baby emotionally, she will miss these dramatic changes because she could not bear to be there through the more subtle ones. Have you ever looked into the night sky for a shooting star or meteor shower? If you get bored and look away, you'll probably miss the show.

PART 3

CHANGING
THE CONVERSATION

CHAPTER 9

Why Don't We Value Mothering?

What's Feminism Got to Do with It?

I was at a dinner party recently where a woman—we'll call her Patty—accused me of being antifeminist. I was really taken aback; I've always thought of myself as a feminist. When I asked why, she told me that criticizing daycare and advocating for women to stay with their children as long as possible before they turn three was antifeminist.

I don't agree. I strongly believe that women and men should have the equal opportunities and choices, and receive equal pay for equal work. I'm thrilled that, as a result of the tireless efforts of feminists, a woman can choose to work and support herself, that she can choose not to marry or to have children (and I do believe that not all women should have children), and that a man is not considered less manly if he expresses his feminine side by wanting to stay home with his children or spend more time caring for them. I believe women and men can work and have children if they put their children first in every way. Yes, I may be child-centric, but that doesn't make me antifeminist.

In an interview in *Garage* magazine, Beyoncé, Queen Bey—who I can safely say is at the top of her profession as a singer and entertainer—said, "Of everything I've accomplished, my proudest moment hands down is when I gave birth to my daughter Blue."[1] Cue the firestorm of criticism. On mic.com, Jenny Kutner reacted: "Wouldn't it be refreshing for one of the most professionally accomplished women in the world to value her career accomplishments equally?"[2] To which Elizabeth Kiefer on Refinery29 responded: "It would be if that were the truth for whoever spoke that perfect soundbite of progressivism. Yet it would be even more refreshing if we allowed women to choose their greatest moment without fear that they were being judged against some ever-moving metric of what it means to be a good feminist."[3] To which I say: Amen.

If being a feminist means you can do whatever you want without considering the consequences to your children of your absence, that you can act without empathy for your child regarding the pain of their separation from you, then I guess I am not a feminist as Patty defines it. The feminists of the 1970s were committed to giving women *choices*, to choose a more career-oriented life and have the same opportunities and salaries and power in the work world as men. Feminism has freed women to make choices, to be independent, to fight abuse, to feel empowered in a world where they often felt disempowered sexually and intellectually, and it has almost leveled the playing field for women and men in terms of career choices and money-making ability. It has also legitimized the option of choosing not to have children. Many of the early feminist leaders chose a life of work and linear professional ambition over having children. That was their choice, and I respect it. But women can't do everything. Men can't do everything. We all make choices, and there is always a path not taken. Having those choices means not that we *should* but that we *can* if we want to. Many mothers must work to support their families. But the lines about what we want and what we need have become blurred. Instead of valuing and prioritizing the relationships with our children, many women race back to work or away from their babies.

In his book *Affect Regulation Theory*, Daniel Hill, psychoanalyst and neurobiologist, said, "The importance of attachment and the relationship with the mother in this critical window of development for the emotional well-being of the child just makes sense when you think about it." There is so much resistance to the debate on maternity leave from inside the ranks of feminists because of the conflict within the ranks of women about having it all without compromise. Important developmental psychologists like Margaret Mahler, Jay Belsky, and the father of attachment, John Bowlby, have been called antifeminists by the same women they seek to help because they have advocated for the rights of children and for their positions on the importance of mothering. In the 1980s, Belsky questioned whether institutionalized daycare was really a good choice for childcare and was labeled a misogynist. So you could say I am in good company with my colleagues who have been mislabeled as antifeminist.

In an op-ed piece in the *New York Times*, Judith Shulevitz wrote,

We need another feminism. . . . Let's call it, for lack of a better term, "caregiverism." It would demand dignity and economic justice for parents dissatisfied with a few weeks of unpaid parental leave, and strive to mitigate the sacrifices made by adult children responsible for aging parents. . . . We're fighting for 12 weeks of leave when we need to rethink the basic chronology of our lives. . . . A caregiverist agenda should include stretching career paths across that longer life span, making it easier for parents of both sexes to dip in and out of the work force as the need arises.[4]

I do not believe you can have it all, or at least not at the same time in life.

First of all, *having* is a possessive word. When we focus on *having* a baby, *having* a marriage, *having* a great and successful job, and *having* lots of material stuff we have lost touch with the most important part of life: *being*. Having a successful career and making lots of money that allows you to buy more stuff doesn't help you to be more present for the ones we love: children, spouses, family, and friends. Intimacy requires time; giving up your role as a primary caregiver comes with sacrificing physical and emotional intimacy with your child.

Anne-Marie Slaughter and her husband were interviewed on CNN. Slaughter's husband raised their two sons as the primary care-giver when Slaughter commuted between Princeton and Washington, where she worked at the State Department. She said, "Now my boys reach out to their father more and text him, not me and it makes me feel very competitive." Her husband said, "That is the benefit of being the primary parent."[5]

Mark, the stay-at-home dad we met in Chapter 6, agrees. He knows he sacrificed some of his earning capacity but never regrets what he gave up in return for his closer relationship to his children.

Life is long, and you can do many things, but you cannot do them all well at the same time. Young women who have been pushed their entire lives to achieve at a high level tell me that if they step off the corporate ladder they can never get back on at the same level. That's true; you may never be the CEO of the bank or corporate law firm if you choose to make your family your first priority. But you may not have emotionally healthy children or have a close relationship with your children now or when they're adults if you make your career your first priority. Someone once wisely said, "When your children are eighteen they get to decide whether they want to know you." And that depends largely on your relationship with them when they are young.

What's also true is that life is not linear, and the most interesting adventures happen when you get off the beaten track. My oldest sister (who is also a psychoanalyst) used to intentionally get lost with her car in an attempt to find alternative routes home. I think this is a good analogy for life and a better model of finding the right mix of personal and professional satisfaction, on our own terms.

I look at women like Congresswoman Nita Lowey, who said, "You can have many careers in your lifetime. . . . I stayed home to raise my children until my youngest was nine years old, and then I went into public service." Elected to Congress in 1988, she still represents New York as of this book's publication.

Katy told me, "It's interesting, because I was very much a late starter with my career, and people are shocked when they hear how far I got."

Katy graduated from Williams College. Married in her twenties to an executive whose job required him to move frequently (they moved ten times in fifteen years of marriage), she had two children. Because they moved so often, Katy devoted her time to caring for her family, occasionally taking a part-time job once the children were in school, and eventually getting her masters of business administration (MBA).

When her children were in middle school, her husband took early retirement to become a consultant, and househusband. They settled in a suburb of Chicago, and Katy found a full-time job at an e-commerce company, then left to take a job as a part-time receptionist at a university, which offered a substantial tuition break to employees' children; her older daughter attended that school. When her younger child started college, Katy was offered a challenging position at a marketing company, managing high-volume corporate accounts. She dove in, and found her maturity, confidence, and life experience gave her an advantage dealing with clients. "I know I took an unpopular path," she said, "But I think there are lessons there that I wish other women would understand."

I have always believed that part of our strength as women is in being more nurturing, empathic, more sensitive emotionally, and more attuned to the nuances of relationships than most men. There has been a new call for women to be leaders in the corporate world, in business, and in politics, but our strength as leaders begins at home with our ability to feel for and nurture our own children.

At some point, women who loved nurturing their children and saw it as a great contribution to society and a meaningful pursuit in life, were told they were not modern, not feminist, not cool if they chose to stay home with their children. Instead of showing respect and admiration for mothers who chose raising a family as their meaningful work, society rejected these women and the meaning of their work. Even their spouses questioned the value of mothering.

I often hear working mothers say how great it is for young women to see their mothers in high-powered careers. That may be true, but when it comes to babies and toddlers, they don't care if their mother has a career; they just care that Mom is there when they need her. When children are older and need their mothers less intensely and they can make sense of their mother's absence, seeing their mother balance meaningful work with raising a family can be empowering. But in the first three years, it's quite a different story.

To create a paradigm shift, our society had to move very far away from the old model to create space for the new one. When you create change, it is often necessary to push away aggressively from where you started, but this new extreme is not meant to be permanent, like an adolescent who declares his independence from his parents dramatically before finding his way back to a new more adult relationship. But instead of finding a way to accommodate and validate a variety of lifestyles and choices, the movement to free women from the fetters of an unequal, choiceless society became a mandate to abandon and denigrate all biological and emotional ties to traditionally female pursuits and professions, including mothering. The time has come for the pendulum to find a healthy resting point between the extremes. All childraising choices should be acceptable, but it's up to the individuals making these choices to understand the responsibilities and ramifications of their decisions.

I would never want to go back to a place where women don't have the choice to live the lives they want for themselves. I dream of a society where women are aware of and honest with themselves about their fears and where, if they do have children, they are able to structure their lives to be with their children when they need them the most and find fulfillment in work, or whatever is important to them, when those children's needs change. Aristotle suggested that lying on our deathbeds, we ask ourselves what in our lives will have given us real satisfaction. At the end of their lives, these women will have passed Aristotle's deathbed test for having lived a good life.

Why Do We Belittle the Nurturing Professions?

In the distant past, cultures glorified the power of giving and nurturing life. Today many women see themselves as warriors in the pursuit of power, money, and work equality and have turned away from nurturing as too soft and without substance. And yet they miss the point that mothering is the concrete foundation of the house that withstands the storms later. Becoming a stronger woman has come to mean being like a man and delegating mothering to strangers who are condescended to, paid low wages, and given little job security and little respect. Many of these caregivers leave their own children to care for others' children, a painful choice that many would dearly love to avoid.

As more lucrative opportunities in traditionally male-dominated fields have opened, more women have turned away from the nurturing professions like teaching, counseling, nursing, speech and physical therapy, massage therapy, and nutrition, which traditionally have given them flexibility and more control over their lives. The problem is that professions like the law, finance, business management, tech, and even being a physician are not usually family friendly, and to compete with men, women have to make work their priority. Fear has replaced control: fear of loss of a job, fear of loss of a "spot" at work, fear of having less money, and fear of loss of self, which is often intensely connected to work. In many industries, work is more like a pair of golden handcuffs. Instead of challenging the status quo, women have bought in hook, line, and sinker. This is in spite of the fact that new research from Cornell University has found that when women enter a field in large numbers, the pay declines for the same job that men were doing before. This occurs not just in jobs that require more education—female physicians make 71 percent of what male physicians earn—but in jobs that require less skill—janitors earn more than maids and housekeepers.[6] Women's work, no matter what that work is, simply isn't valued as highly.

In a *New York Times* article in September 2015, Joan Williams, director of the Center for WorkLife Law at the University of California, Hastings, said, "The underlying work culture sends the message that if you're really committed, you're here all the time."[7] Look at Yahoo!: In 2013, the company lengthened its maternity leave policy, but CEO Marissa Mayer took only a two-week leave after giving birth to twins. What kind of message does this send to female employees?

Success has become tied to financial, professional, and material endeavors rather than relationships, and the 24/7 workplace has replaced the value of mothering as a priority. According to a Pew Research study from 2009, 37 percent of women with children prefer to work full-time, and 62 percent prefer to work part-time.[8] Ambivalence about nurturing and the importance of being a mother as a priority over paid labor is a very disturbing statistic. A handful of economists may tell us that women working benefits society economically, but what is good for the economy is not necessarily good for society emotionally.

A long-term longitudinal study on happiness and living a good life at Harvard University followed 724 men over seventy-seven years to understand what makes people happy. The conclusion: It wasn't money, power, and fame that made people happy, but relationships.[9] My oldest son returned from an internship in South Africa. Working to deliver healthcare services to poor youth living with AIDS inspired him with a passion to help and to give to those less fortunate than himself. He said to me, "Mom, I saw people with so little and yet their values were on relationships, family, friends, and community. . . . It is the most important part of their lives." I think this says it all.

Maternity leave policies and the lack of flexible work options obviously affect when and in what capacity women return to work after having a baby. But if 37 percent of women *choose* to return to work full-time as quickly as possible after their child is born, it is not just an *external* obstacle we face, but an *internal* one as women.

Charlotte, a mother of three, who decided not to return to her job as a magazine editor after her second child was born, told me, "I love staying home. I wouldn't feel any conflict if society didn't tell me it was wrong. Wherever you turn, society tells stay-at-home moms that we are not contributing to society or we are less than working mothers; that's part of the problem, if you ask me. When my children need me, when the school calls, I want to be the one to comfort them. Not a nanny, not my mother-in-law, but *me*. I felt that way when they were babies, and I feel that way now that they are older. If only society would recognize our value."

It is not impossible to work in male-dominated professions, where the work culture bleeds into home life, but it requires courage of conviction, persistent assertion of need, and a commitment to setting boundaries at work and at home. It also requires the willingness to lose some—or sometimes all—of the progress you have made in your career to get what you and your family need.

I've interviewed mothers, like Mara in Chapter 4, who work in fields that are less mother friendly and have made it work for them, but the "female" helping professions are still the best jobs for women who want to be as present for their children as possible in the early years from a logistical perspective. It is also worth mentioning that these professions are more in line with the work of raising children from an emotional perspective. If you have been working all day in a profession that requires left-brain skills and promotes aggressive, competitive, unempathic behavior, it is more difficult at the end of the day to shift gears and turn on your right-brain empathy and sensitivity.

I met a young pediatrician at a conference. She worked at a very prestigious hospital on the East Coast. "You won't believe it," she told me, "but pediatricians, who are in the business of caring for children's mental and physical well-being, are given two weeks off from their work for maternity leave. It was terrible how I knew it was best to be home with my child, but I had to return to work or lose my position." I asked her if she had thought about leaving her job, and she said she had, but was too frightened—where would she go and what would she do? I was furious: She had to go to work and advocate for women to stay home with their children when she could not do so herself? Ironic, isn't it?

The Economics of Nurturing

I cannot discuss the devaluing of mothering as an occupation without mentioning our society's prioritization of economics over the emotional health of our children and future generations. Making money has become our litmus test for success, and relationships have become secondary to material and professional achievements. A recent survey of millennials asked them for their most important life goals. Over 80 percent said to get rich and another 50 percent was to become famous.[10] Maybe that is why we have such a crisis of unhappy, depressed, and anxious adults in America, where we focus on material wealth and status. We do not value mothering and nurturing as meaningful work when compared with paid work outside the home. Many of the studies that say women should go back to work are authored by economists rather than therapists, who do not see the impact of a mother's absence on her very young children and encourage (whether they mean to or not) a detached approach to raising children. Freud said we need "love and work" to be happy, but note in what order those words appear; as the saying goes, no one on their deathbed ever said, "I should have spent more time at the office." Will we regret that we didn't get another promotion or that we didn't accumulate enough wealth or status or will we regret feeling alone and disconnected from those we should be most intimate with? Will our children mourn us? Will we leave them emotionally healthy as our legacy or with a pain and emptiness in their hearts where love and security should have been? Will we be (as we say in Judaism) a "blessing in their memory" or a curse because of our neglect?

> Making money has become our litmus test for success.

After World War II, our society became more focused on the accumulation of material wealth and possessions. Having the newest, the biggest, the best of anything became a national obsession. New professional opportunities opened for women. At some point, the women's movement, which began by advocating for equal treatment and pay under the law and the right to make whatever life choices were best for each woman, took the position that a woman would not be fulfilled or satisfied unless she worked outside the home, no matter how young her children were. In this paradigm women had more choices and more control over their own money, but they also felt the withdrawal of societal support and respect for the work of nurturing relationships and the helping professions. Many women who chose to work and delegate the care of their children to others looked down on women who chose to be their children's primary caregiver or opted for the mommy track at work. We threw the baby out with the bath water, almost literally.

Our economy and way of life have become dependent on two-income working families. According to the Pew Research Center, the number of dual-income households in America has risen from 25 percent in 1960 to 60 percent in 2012, and continues to rise.[11] If you live in New York City (and not just Manhattan) you cannot go a week or two without hearing someone say it is so hard to live comfortably if both parents are not working. Many of my clients are in the upper-middle and upper-income brackets, and mothers who come to see me often tell me that they and their husbands or spouses *must* work full-time to make ends meet. My first question after that statement is how much of that is *need* and how much is *desire*? If you and your partner must both work to pay the bills for food, shelter, medical care, transportation, and clothing, that's need. If you're both working so you can afford a BMW and sixty-inch flat screen, that's desire. A family with two working parents may make sense financially, but it may also come at the expense of the children's well-being. It comes with other more tangible costs as well. After all the additional expenses—commuting, clothing, paying for services (cleaning, take-out), and, most important, childcare, the actual financial benefits may not be as big as you think. Depending on where you live, an in-home caregiver, can cost up to $700 a week, not including additional costs for insurance and taxes. Daycare, often the least expensive option, can cost from $330 to $1,564 a month, with fees for early drop-off and late pickup. In 2013, Salary .com estimated that it would take more than $113,586 a year to replace the most important tasks a mother handles,[12] and those costs continue to rise.

Even our political and business leaders, many of whom are women, continue to promote the idea that full-time work is more admirable and fulfilling than raising our children, that cost-effective daycare is an acceptable and even desirable form of caregiving for very young children, and that we can do it all and don't have to sacrifice anything to become successful professionally and financially. We are told by society that women making money is better for society and better for us and even better for our families than being with our children. Yes, there is a benefit for a family to have more financial resources, and (and this is an important point) as children get older, a working mother shows her children that women can achieve as much as men, but this is not the whole truth.

All women should have the right to be with their children when they are young. However, there are exceptions to the working versus staying home cost–benefit analysis for mothers and babies. Studies have shown that children of working-class single mothers who work regular hours, and even shift schedules, are better off in terms of their mental health because of the advantages of financial security that the mother's work brings to her family. In low-income families, lessening the family's financial burden also reduces the mother's stress. However, the same studies have shown that children of two-parent working middle-class and upper-middle-class families do *less* well in terms of their mental health when both parents work, and even worse when their mother does shift work or works more than eight hours a day, as many professions today require. My experience working with children in affluent families is that these children understand that their mothers and fathers prefer to prioritize work and career and material success over them. They feel their parents' detachment and interpret it as rejection. Children are the greatest litmus test of our intentions. They know when we are truly sorry that we cannot be with them and when we would rather be somewhere else. I've found that young children are wiser and more in touch with the most important things, like relationships, intimacy, dependency, and the nature of love as a priority.

In her book *The Price of Privilege*, Madeleine Levine described how the American culture of affluence, in which objects have replaced intimacy, has created a generation of young people who lack an authentic sense of self.[13] She deals primarily with teenagers, but as we've seen, building that secure internal structure begins much, much earlier.

Yes, there is a benefit for mothers who must work to provide for their children financially out of real need. And yet the research always weighs the benefit to these women in relation to the stress that not having money causes. However, this paradigm does not exist in middle-, upper-middle-, and upper-class families because there is less financial stress before the mother chooses to work. A study of mothers who are under the poverty line shows that 56 percent suffered from postpartum depression. We have no such statistics for women of professional or wealthy classes, yet I have seen an increase of mothers with postpartum depression in my practice. In fact, adding very intense work or very long hours of work outside the home to an upper-middle-class mother's life adds more stress to both the mother's life and that of her family.

It is easy to get confused over what we want versus what we need. When we teach our toddlers about why they cannot have a new toy every day, we are essentially teaching them that they cannot have everything they want and that they must learn to tolerate frustration and distinguish what is necessary from what is desired. It is the same dilemma for mothers who must distinguish between what is really important for their children and for their families and what they wish for. If you want to work because you love your work and love making money, but you need to care for your child, maybe the compromise is to work, but work fewer hours or to work at a job that doesn't demand you to be available when you're not in the office. If, however, your solution is to focus on your needs alone because society tells you that your continued and consistent presence isn't necessary for your children to grow up to be healthy, loving, responsible adults, then you aren't making a fully informed choice.

> **It is easy to get confused over what we want versus what we need.**

CHAPTER 10

Where Do We Go from Here?

Making the Needs of Families a Priority

Changing Policy

I'm not an economist or a policy wonk. I don't claim to have all the figures that can make the statistical case that when women stay home it's better not just for their families but for society too. What I do have is experience on the front lines of treating mothers who are dealing with the consequences of putting work or other interests before the well-being of their babies and young children and of seeing children who are suffering because their mothers are not present for them in a meaningful way.

The Family and Medical Leave Act of 1993 requires covered employers (some employers are exempt) to allow eligible employees to take a job-protected, *unpaid* leave of up to twelve weeks to deal with a serious health condition of themselves, a parent, spouse/partner, or child; for pregnancy or care of a newborn child (within one year of birth), or for adoption or foster care of a child.[1] This is not maternity leave. Some would argue that in an ideal world, companies would offer a year of paid maternity leave, with a second year of part-time or flexible hours. I would like to see the United States institute a policy of six months' leave at full pay, six months' leave at partial pay, and the ability to have a flexible work schedule for the next two years. While no country offers that solution, a 2014 International Labor Organization report pointed out that the United States is one of only three countries that does not guarantee some kind of paid leave for new parents.[2] Paid leave has undeniable benefits, including lower mortality rates for mothers and babies. A Norwegian study found that children born after 1977, when the government began allowing mothers four months of paid and twelve months of unpaid leave, had lower rates of dropping out of school, higher rates of college attendance, and higher incomes as adults than children born before 1977, before the law was enacted.[3]

The onus for implementing *paid* leave has fallen on individual companies. Some are rising to the challenge, like Etsy, whose revised policy offers all corporate employees (that is, not the sellers) twenty-six weeks of paid leave. This includes adoptive parents and those who become parents via surrogacy. "We want to build a culture where all parents—regardless of gender—are equally encouraged and supported to take time to care for their new and growing families."[4] As I write this, it remains to be seen how the policy will be used, but it's a hopeful sign when a company understands that what's good for families is good for business. I hope other companies take note, and follow suit.

Other companies and institutions are not so compassionate and forward thinking. Joan is an African American teacher of social justice at a prestigious private school. When she was pregnant with her son, the school gave her a twelve-week maternity leave, nine of which were paid; the first two weeks of her leave were the last two weeks of her pregnancy. Though she wanted to extend her leave and was willing to do so without pay, the school wouldn't agree to this. Returning to work so soon after the birth of her son was so painful, that when she was pregnant with her daughter, she arranged to take a leave of absence for a year. She assumed that nine weeks would be paid, as it had been with her previous leave, but because she was taking a leave of absence, her maternity leave was not covered. "We take care of other people's children," she said, "But the school doesn't prioritize family over the institution."

While paid leave is a popular talking point for politicians and pundits, if women feel conflicted about their role as their children's most important caregiver and continue to put their ambition first, then how can we advocate for policies that are in the best interests of our children? How can we expect that our government and societal institutions will make appropriate changes to a broken system? Until we accept that there is no more important work than raising emotionally healthy human beings, those policies are unlikely to change.

Women's Ambivalence: Changing the Culture

Until we resolve our ambivalence over whether nurturing is valuable work, and is an asset to society at large, we will not approach the kind of policy for maternity leave (which takes place immediately after the birth or adoption of a child) or for home care leave (which extends the time a woman can spend caring for her infant or child) in America that equals that of countries in eastern and northern Europe, which offer a combination of full and partial paid leave. Some countries offer up to 166 weeks of total leave for new mothers. Societal support for this kind of legislation will require that we recognize that the healthcare costs—in terms of money; of generations of ill and underfunctioning children; and of young adults who suffer from depression, anxiety, and addictions of all kinds—outweigh the economic benefits of women working when their children are very young plus the cost of paid maternity leave. There has been an increase of 400 percent in mental illness in children and adolescents in the past decade.[5] If our children are the litmus test of the health of a society, then it's clear that something is wrong.

From 1995 to 1997, Kaiser Permanente conducted the groundbreaking Adverse Childhood Experience Survey. Given to more than 17,000 participants, from all social and economic backgrounds, it clearly showed the connection between neglect, abuse, and stress in childhood and later negative mental and physical health outcomes, such as depression, anxiety, and addiction, heart issues, diabetes, and cancer.[6] These health issues cost society not only in dollars for medical support services but in human capital due to lost labor.

In addition to the loss of healthy young adults, the workforce is also losing women who, if paid maternity leave and the flexibility to work part-time were available, would be more likely to continue working after their children were born. To date, only 12 percent of American workers have paid leave to care for a baby or sick relative,[7] but companies are recognizing that if they are going to retain female talent they have to be generous with maternity leave. The Virgin Group and Netflix recently extended paid leave to a year for new parents.[8] YouTube CEO Susan Wojcicki noted that in 2007, when parent company Google increased maternity leave from twelve weeks to eighteen weeks, it halved the rate at which new mothers quit.[9]

According to the Center for American Progress, it costs businesses 20 percent or more of an employee's salary to replace him or her.[10] In her book *Unfinished Business*, Anne-Marie Slaughter pointed out that a country without maternity leave and flexible work hours for mothers pushes many women either to abandon their children to the care of others when they would rather not do so or to abandon their work.[11]

The corporate and professional worlds are missing an opportunity to retain talented women who, if given the choice, would remain involved in their careers, even if they lowered their intensity in the early years of raising their children. Many women are driven away from their chosen professions because they are either denied the freedom to regulate their work and time away from home when their children are young or are denied the guarantee of keeping their positions if they recognize the importance of taking time off after having a baby.

Just as babies can hold it together for only a limited number of hours when separated from their mothers, women too have an expiration date on the amount of time they can be away from their babies. A new mother who is given the opportunity to work part-time may be hungrier to prove herself valuable and may be more productive than a mother who works full-time and feels guilty and conflicted about leaving her child for many hours every day. And the woman with reduced work hours is more likely to be loyal to an employer who gives her the support and flexibility she needs.

Compromise in our careers in the short run means long-term satisfaction with our most important assets, our children. We need to start thinking of compromise as freedom, not prison. While there are laws that protect women from losing their jobs entirely when they take maternity leave, it may not mean that they reenter their careers at precisely

> We need to start thinking of compromise as freedom, not prison.

the same level or with the same intensity if they hope to have control over their schedules to give more to their children. This may lead women down wonderfully satisfying paths they may not have taken if they had not been diverted by motherhood.

Embracing Shifting Roles and New Family Structures

The old paradigms of what a family is or is not have changed. We need to recognize the importance of the role of fathers in caregiving and encourage the acceptance of alternative family models. However, we must also acknowledge emotional challenges of these new models for a child and reconcile the losses that these alternatives represent to our children, rather than denying them. A child may be raised by a single mother or father, or two mothers, or two fathers. There are still not enough long-term studies to help us understand how these alternative family models will impact children's psyche and mental health, but the preliminary models suggest that if children are given sensitive nurturing, they can thrive. But for any of these alternative family models to work, it is necessary to not lose sight of the importance of mothers and the role they play, even when they are not involved or are not present.

Fatherhood is changing. Almost a third of American women outearn their husbands, and more men share in the tasks of caring for their children and running the household. The number of men who stay home while their spouse works has grown: almost 2 million according to a 2014 Pew Research Center Study, and more than 20 percent of those men are there specifically to care for their children.[12]

For fathers to be effective primary caregivers, they have to learn to be more like mothers in terms of how they relate to, care for, and are emotionally present for their babies. We know that when fathers spend more time with their children their levels of oxytocin rise, making it more likely that they will become more sensitive nurturers. Fathers can also be taught to nurture more like sensitive mothers, like Mark, whom we met in Chapter 6. Who knows how this will eventually change fathers' brains?

The other issue for fathers who are caring for their children full-time is recognizing and acknowledging the loss of the mother for the child. This means allowing the child to mourn the loss of their mothers as their primary nurturer and express their sadness and/or anger without feeling rejected or upset or angry themselves.

When two gay men are raising a child, it is equally important that the loss or absence of a mother is acknowledged. Every child has a biological mother and a fantasy of the mother he wishes he had; the mysteries of who their child's mother is and where she is must be addressed as well as the child's feelings of confusion, sadness, disappointment, and anger. Before the age of two, a child can't ask that question directly, but she does feel that loss. If all her other needs are met (she's not hungry, wet, or uncomfortable), and she is still crying, it's possible that is the cause. Sensitive comforting is called for (see Chapters 4 and 5).

When a child begins to speak, she will ask, "Why don't I have a mother?" The answer should *not* automatically be, "You don't have a mother but you have two loving fathers"; instead, ask how she feels about not having a mother. Let her know it's okay if that makes her feel sad or angry. A child should feel that she can ask this question without being afraid that she will upset her parents or make them angry. Let her express her curiosity, upset, or disappointment over not having a mother; it doesn't mean she loves her fathers any less.

We can no longer deny the harm that our work-before-family mind-set is inflicting on the emotional and mental health of our children. Whether we are talking about mothers who rarely see their children or fathers who are away much of the time, the absence of present parents is creating a generation of lost and emotionally damaged children. The dual-income family is a societal norm, and sometimes a necessity, but we have lost sight of the values of family first in favor of material success.

Our society constantly sends us contradictory messages. We want to eradicate mental health issues like depression, anxiety, and violence in children and young adults but don't really want to look too deeply at the root of the problem. We say we value family, but we work longer hours and take less vacation time than any other country in the world. We still promote having families even when we cannot care for them; working 24/7 is not in harmony with raising healthy children. Even when parents are offered paid maternity and paternity leave, many do not take advantage of it. A recent article in Fast Company explained Amazon's innovative new maternity leave policy, which offers up to twenty weeks of parental leave for birth mothers, and a "leave-share" program that enables employees to share their leave with their partner, who may not get paid parental leave. They also created the Ramp Back program, which gives new mothers and primary caregivers eight weeks of flexible time.[13] But—and it's a big *but*—many employees do not take the leave because they fear of the loss of their jobs or, worse, the loss of their status in their jobs. The *culture* itself has to change so women feel these policies offer real choices, without strings attached or negative consequences.

> Working 24/7 is not in harmony with raising healthy children.

Changing a culture begins at home, and inside each of us. It begins with accepting that when you have a baby *everything* changes, including the importance of work in your life. This means whoever is taking on the role of primary parent is going to be less involved in work and more involved in their child. Too many women buy into the fantasy that they will not need to compromise on the level or intensity of their work after they have a baby; if they plan to be emotionally present for their baby, that's simply not realistic.

Shifting priorities or rebalancing our lives does not mean that we go back to business as usual after we have a baby. Change may be the result of our own efforts to reduce our responsibilities and the hours we spend at our jobs in the critical three-year window of our baby's development. Change may come from an employer who offers a realistic re-entry timeline and program for women returning to work after maternity leave. You cannot expect your job will be held in suspended animation for you while you are away, just as you cannot believe your baby remains in a state of suspended animation waiting for you to arrive home after ten hours at work. The traditional corporate structure doesn't offer women the control and flexible schedules they need when this shift in priorities happens. Even companies founded and/or run by women still, for the most part, follow the old rules and have the same expectations. If companies won't accommodate the realities of a mother's needs, then we can create our own opportunities. Women are natural entrepreneurs, and the skills we have, in whatever field we have expertise, can be exploited for our own benefit. We are our own best bosses when we are raising children. The benefits package may not be as generous as a corporate one, but you don't have to ask permission to take the time to be with your child.

No matter how understanding we expect individual companies to be regarding maternity leave for all their employees, the law must also protect women who are at high socioeconomic risk. Many women work on an hourly basis or work in low-paying shift jobs. They are not worrying about whether they will be able to take their vacation that year or whether they'll get a bonus; they are worrying about how they will pay the rent and grocery bills so their children have the basics of living. It is an obligation, not a choice, to provide for those less fortunate and with fewer opportunities. It is our responsibility and obligation, through our federal government, to enact laws that protect these women in the workplace, including some kind of paid maternity leave and income subsidies that would allow them to have more options about how many hours they need to work without worrying about whether they can provide food and shelter for their children. We must implement new policies that support the needs of *all* mothers—no matter what their socioeconomic position—to work less intensely and part-time so they can be more available to their children.

All mothers need more support so they can mother. Women are expected to shoulder the day-to-day tasks of running a household, be the primary caregiver, and be the logistical and emotional center of the family, even if they work outside the home (or have a home-based business). It is impossible to do everything that is expected of us without the support of family, friends, employers, and the government. At one time, women had a literal village around them, a tight-knit community of kin and neighbors; that's not the case today.

Businesses are allowed to offer employees tax-free saving accounts for childcare; why not offer tax breaks to a grandmother, sister, or aunt who will help a mother care for her children? Social innovator Mark Freedman, CEO and founder of Encore.org, has suggested that as we live longer and are able to work longer, women should be able to tap into Social Security when they take time from work to raise their children. For each year they use Social Security before their official retirement age, they would defer their retirement age. He also believes that our elders are underutilized and can take a bigger role supporting mothers.

There are some legislators who are advocating for mothers and families. Congresswoman Nita Lowey is a strong supporter of paid maternity leave: "We talk a lot about family values but need to back it up with reality . . . taking care of an infant or caring for a loved one is extraordinarily important work." She has proposed the Social Security Caregiver Credit Act, which would provide Social Security credits for women who take time off to raise young children or care for an elderly or sick parent.[14] Senator Kirsten Gillibrand and Congresswoman Rosa DeLauro introduced the Family and Medical Insurance Leave Act in 2013, which would create a national insurance program funded equally by employer and employee contributions. The program would provide workers who are insured for disability insurance benefits under the Social Security Act twelve weeks or sixty workdays of paid leave while they care for a newborn or ill family member.[15] It is not enough, but it is a start.

We have to learn to ask for help from others: our mothers or mothers-in-law, female relatives, babysitters, friends, and other mothers but especially our spouses or partners. Today, it's fathers who play the most critical role in supporting mothers, particularly when both partners must work. What does this mean? That if your children are going to be your first priority, then your spouse or partner has to become a more equal partner in sharing the care of the household, including providing meals, cleaning the cat box or walking the dog, and vacuuming the floor.

Even if a partner is already a willing (if not enthusiastic) participant, cook, or housecleaner, the most important way fathers can support mothers is to encourage them to make the choices that are best for them and their families, admire them, and respect them for doing what is the most important work in the world, that of being present emotionally and physically for their young children even at the expense of additional financial security.

From the Mouths of Teens

I recently spoke with a group of young men and women, sixteen and seventeen years old, about some of the issues in this book that they said were important to them. These young people are our future, and it was a fascinating exercise that both saddened me and gave me hope.

Though they were a little hesitant to admit it, most of these teens said that while their dads were great, their moms were unique and special to them in a different way. David said, "Fathers are a really important lost resource, but isn't it better to have one parent who is very nurturing and one who helps the child to separate and be resilient?" Jenna told me, "My mother is more nurturing than my father; it seems like it's a biological impulse for mothers to show affection and nurture. It doesn't mean either parent loves you less: My mom will respond with how do you feel and how does the other person feel, while my dad is less interested in feelings and just wants to know I am okay."

Many of the teens expressed feeling close to their mothers, especially the ones who had been physically and emotionally available when they were young. Samantha remembered how her friends would come to her mom for advice. She said, "I was so grateful I had a mom so much of the time and [one] whom I felt so close to." The sadness was apparent in those kids whose mothers were not as present. James, whose mother wasn't as available, said, "I feel angry at my mom and feel closer to my dad because he was around for me."

The conflicts the young women felt were clear. Some of the young women expressed concern that by making their children a priority, rather than work, they were betraying feminist principles. Though almost all of them acknowledged that mothering is more important than paid labor and important to the emotional well-being of children, the young women were worried about being judged for choosing to stay home with their (potential) children rather than pursue a career while they were raising a family. "What could be more interesting than your children?" asked Karen, whose mother stayed home to raise her family, "I don't want to mess up having children," she went on. "Mothering is definitely more important than paid work." On the other hand, Jane declared, "I find myself discrediting women who choose to stay home with their children as antifeminist. I hate that I do this, but I find myself judging them. So how will this impact my choices?"

Everyone agreed that quality time was not a replacement for quantity time, and that you cannot be present emotionally if you are not physically present enough as well. Some of their comments:

"Quality time causes stress and anxiety."

"You cannot artificially create quality time; it can't replace spending time together."

"Parents try to make quality time; most kids resent it because it's on the parents' schedule not on the kid's schedule."

"Saying I love you in a ritualized forced way isn't a substitute for being there; there is no substitute for being there."

"My mom works part-time now, but now is not when I needed her. When I was little that is when I really needed her to be around all the time."

The students knew when their mothers felt badly about having to leave them for work, and when their mothers felt their work was more important than they were. Sofie said, "My mom needs a lot of reassurance and asks that I say 'I love you' a lot, when she feels guilty or insecure. [She] feels guilty even though she stayed home part-time that she didn't provide us with a good role model for being high powered; she's afraid she has been antifeminist with us. It's confusing to me because she is confused about how important her role as a mother was, even though she did prioritize it."

Lilah observed that her mother, who worked extremely long hours and traveled frequently, "has sad and guilty feelings she was not there for us; now she is realizing what she missed, but it's kind of late. She shows us she loves us by buying us good stuff with the money she makes in her job. I know she feels guilty and uses the stuff as a substitute." It was clear when Lilah spoke that "stuff" as a substitute for her mother's presence just didn't cut it.

How did they feel about their own futures, work, and family? What were their concerns? Sofie wondered, "If my husband will understand if I want to raise my children or will it cause marital problems." And Jenna thought, "Working is a good thing and I think you can learn a great deal from working, but I am concerned I will not be able to strike a balance and be a good enough mom."

When these young men and women are ready to have children of their own, I hope the world will have become a more compassionate and welcoming place for all mothers. But for all of us who are here now, my wish is that you understand there is no greater gift you can give your child than being as present emotionally and physically in the first three years as possible.

That investment will produce a higher yield than any other investment you will ever make now, and as your children grow up. The rewards may not increase your bank account, but I assure you that you will not regret the decisions you make when you see your children happy, healthy, thriving, and loving.

APPENDIX A

INTERVIEWING A CAREGIVER

When you're interviewing a caregiver, give consideration to body language, trust your gut feeling, and pay attention to the facts. Here are some questions my colleagues and I at Nannies Who Know suggest mothers ask a potential caregiver. The questions are arranged in no particular order, and not all of them will be applicable to your situation.

About a Caregiver's Background

How long have you been caring for children? How old were the children you cared for?

What was your most recent position?

Why are you leaving or why have you left your job?

What were some of the best and the most challenging aspects of your previous job?

Have you ever had to handle an emergency and how did you deal with it?

What is your highest level of education?

Do you have a family of your own?

Where do you live and what are your responsibilities to your own family?

Do you have any special life or work experiences that you would bring to this job?

Are you looking for a long-term job or seeking to pursue another profession/job or education in the next year or few years?

Are you certified in first aid and/or CPR? If you're not, would you be willing to take a course, at our expense?

Have you had negative work situations and what did you learn from them?

What do you like best about being a nanny?

What do find the most challenging about being a nanny?

What do you do in your free time?

What are you looking for in an employer?

Why are you interested in this position?

About Job Responsibilities

How flexible is your schedule? If we need you to come in early or stay late is that possible?

Are you willing to cook, clean, do light housekeeping and laundry, and make playdates?

Are there any responsibilities you like best? And any you will not do?

Would you be willing to travel with our family, stay overnight, or stay with our children for several days if we went away?

How many children are you comfortable watching at once?

What would you do to encourage a child to bond with you?

How do you feel about encouraging play and kids exploring their environment?

How do you think your family or closest friends would describe your personality?

How would you feel working with a stay-at-home mom *or* a mom working many hours outside the home? (Depending on your personal situation.)

How would you deal with a picky eater or a child who refuses to eat?

If you disagreed with my style on discipline, eating, or anything else, how would you handle that?

Do you prefer a more or less structured day?

What is your view of disciplining a child (depending on the age of your children) and what should your role be?

How do you prefer to communicate during the day?

How would you feel about maintaining special diet (gluten free, vegetarian, allergies, kosher)?

How do you feel about working with a special needs child with autism, ADHD, or a spirited or generally challenging child?

Are you comfortable caring for a child with particular medication needs or allergies?

Would you be willing to assist with homework and read books with my child?

What kinds of games and activities do you play with children?

How would handle a child who bites or hits another child? Or hits you?

How do you feel about arranging playdates?

What would you do when a child refuses to clean up or eat? When she has a temper tantrum?

How would you handle a child who is nervous about going to a playdate or birthday party?

What is your approach to toilet training?

What You Cannot Ask a Caregiver Candidate in an Interview

Her age

Her race/ethnic background

Her religious views

Her sexual orientation

Her marital status and if she plans to get pregnant

If she has a disability

If she has been arrested

APPENDIX B

MINDFULNESS EXERCISES

In Chapter 4, I introduced the idea of mindfulness exercises. My thanks to Nancy Fischer Mortifee, who provided them. Mortifee is a mindfulness teacher and workshop facilitator who has worked with adults and children for over thirty years and has studied at many of the major mindfulness institutes including Esalen Institute, Omega Institute, Hollyhock Retreat Center, and Harvard University. She is the coauthor, with John Kehoe, of *Mind Power for Children: A Guide for Parents and Teachers.*

Noticing and Naming Feelings

When we are busy, we may not be conscious of our bodies at all. You can (almost) always count on a few precious moments alone, several times a day, either on the toilet or, when we are really lucky, in the bathtub. Here's how to take advantage of them:

First, notice your breathing: Is it rushed, shallow, all in your chest? Are your shoulders hunched? Can you feel tension anywhere in your body? Maybe everywhere?

Now give a big sigh and let all your energy drop to your bottom. Again, notice how you are breathing and ask yourself, "How am I feeling now?"

Grab a towel, take a few more deep sighs, and yell into the towel.

Towels can take a lot of our energy and no one's feelings get hurt. A few moments of yelling into a towel can reduce the chance of your anger and frustration escalating, and overreacting later.

Give Yourself a Hug

Before you get out of bed in the morning (assuming you haven't been woken by your baby's cries), spend a few quiet moments and wrap your arms around yourself and hug yourself a hug to greet yourself and welcome your body into another day. Remind yourself to be your own best friend, and you are a person separate from your spouse or partner and child.

The Easiest Mindful Breathing Exercise

Sitting comfortably on a chair, a bed, or the floor, with eyes softly closed, breathe through your nose. Notice your breath coming in and going out. There's no need to change anything but the pattern of your breathing—just notice the breath, in and out, in and out.

After a few breaths, breathe in through your nose, consciously open your throat, and follow your breath into your throat. The breath still exits easily through your nose and brings your attention to your throat. Continue for a few breaths at your own rhythm.

On the next inhalation, imagine your breath flowing down through your throat and filling up your chest. Take a few breaths there at your own pace. There's no rush.

On the next inhalation, allow your breath to travel down deeper into your midsection, just above your belly button. Again the breath flows without tension or force, just bringing your attention and awareness to your midsection. Maybe it feels a bit more relaxed as your breath fills this area or not. Just allow the breath to be as it is, without the need to change anything.

On the next inhalation, bring your breath in and let it travel deep into your belly. Imagine filling your belly with this warm breath, noticing how naturally the breath fills your belly and then just as naturally leaves through your nose. Now, as you keep breathing into your belly, gently bring your attention and awareness as deeply into your body as you can. There's nothing to do but notice and keep breathing. Stay here as long as you'd like.

This exercise works like magic when I notice my breath getting short or my mind is all buzzy with thoughts or experiences of anxiety. The important thing to remember is this is the most natural way to breathe and is, in fact, the way our babies breathe, right into their diaphragm.

Breathing Together

Have you ever tried to get your infant or toddler to settle down for a nap when you are feeling desperate, stressed, or frustrated? Mindfully connecting to the breathing of your child and breathing along with her can help relax both you and your baby and get the two of you in sync with each other emotionally.

Sitting or lying next to your child, put your hand on her back or tummy and stroke gently in rhythm with her breath. Even though babies breathe more quickly than adults, try to match your breath to your little one's. Consciously and gradually start to slow your breathing and begin to slow the rate of your stroking to match your breath.

It might seem like this exercise will take too long, especially when you have other things to do. Be patient. Your child will start to breathe more slowly in response to your touch and breathing, and your slower breath and physical closeness to your child will calm your heart and mind.

> **The Following Exercises Are Suitable for
> Children Aged Two or Older**

Soft Belly Breathing

Sit with your toddler facing you. With both hands resting gently on your belly, take a slow deep breath through your nose and softly let the air out through your mouth. Now invite your toddler to join you. Together you can notice how your bellies rise and fall with each breath. Remember, children breathe much faster than adults, so following the rhythm of your child builds a feeling of connection. Notice how calming soft belly breathing is for both you and your child. You can return to this practice whenever some calming moments would be welcome in your day together.

Mindful Listening

This exercise improves the ability to focus and sustain attention for both you and your child. You will need an instrument that can make a sustained sound: a triangle, singing bowl, gong, or bell, for example.

Begin by sitting facing your child. Show her how to place her hands on her lap, with the palms up, just like open ears. Strike the instrument, position your hands like your child's, and listen until you both can no longer hear the sound. When that happens, you each turn your hands over.

Mindful Smelling

Gather several small covered containers or bottles, like vitamin or pill bottles. Infuse cotton balls or pads with a variety of smells like vinegar, perfumes, or an essential oil, and place each cotton ball in its own container. You can use other aromatics like whole spices (cinnamon, cloves), evergreen needles, or citrus peels. Have your child close his eyes and try to identify the smells.

Mindful Eating

We are so concerned about just getting through a meal with our children that we forget that eating can be a delightfully sensuous experience. This exercise lets you model thoughtful and enjoyable eating with your child.

With slightly older children who are not at risk of choking, bite-size foods like raisins, small pieces of fruit like cut-up apples or pears or orange or clementine sections, or fresh berries are perfect for practicing mindful eating. Serve yourself and your child a morsel and take a few moments to enjoy the smell, feel the texture, and notice the color of the fruit in your hand. Ask your child to put the fruit in his mouth and slowly start chewing. You do the same. When you and your child have finished eating, talk about how the fruit smells, tastes, feels. Use as many words as you can to describe the fruit: sweet, crunchy, mushy, squishy.

APPENDIX C

THE GREAT SLEEP CHALLENGE

Getting your children to sleep through the night can be one of the most frustrating, confusing, and exhausting tasks of parenting.

Sleep is one of the most important milestones in a child's development. Popular literature tries to convince parents to adapt a single way to conquer the sleep challenge; for example, the "Ferberizers" and the "Family Bed" believers. The difficulty is not in the philosophies themselves but that every child develops at her own pace and in her own way, and varies in sensitivity.

Much of the literature that talks about creating a sleep routine and training your child to sleep ignores the complex emotional component of sleep, the individuality of your child and circumstances.

It is important to understand *why* your child may have difficulty sleeping. Wakefulness can be the result of an infant needing reassurance that her mother is present. If a mother is away from the child for a large part of the day (whether for work or other reasons), there may be a correlation between a child's wakefulness and her desire to have her mother's full attention at night.

Learning to fall asleep, stay asleep, and fall back to sleep when awakened is a matter of habit, and bad habits can be broken if you pay attention to your individual child's cues. The problem with the strict behavioral "make them cry it out" sleep methods is that they often promote "training" too young and ignore the nuance of the cries.

Children may cry out of need, want, or desperation. It is a parent's role to be sensitive to the difference in a child's cry and the point at which you try to habitualize sleep, which is usually not before six or eight months, and may in some cases be later.

There are many factors that affect a child's ability to sleep—illness, room temperature, a change in routine, emotional upset, physical pain (teething or illness), or even discomfort from a too-tight diaper or scratchy pajamas. Basically, the only thing that is consistent regarding sleep and young children is inconsistency. The good news is that your child will eventually outgrow her wakefulness once she feels emotionally secure, and once the teething, potty training, speech, and movement hurdles have been crossed.

In the meantime, you may find the following suggestions helpful:

- Don't introduce sleep/separation frustration too young. Don't try to sleep train your child until she is *at least* six or eight months old. Even then, assess your child's cries and meet her need for contact and comfort until she is old enough to comfort herself. Pay attention to your child, not the books (or other well-meaning advice).

- Introduce frustration in small doses. If two or three minutes of crying doesn't help your baby settle down, don't torture her, or yourself. Go in to comfort and reassure her, then leave again and wait a few more minutes. If the crying continues check on her again, using your words and touch to reassure her. Remind her that you will be near her if she needs you, and that it is okay to fall asleep. If her crying persists for more than five minutes, it is probably too early to use this approach with your child. Try again in a few weeks. As children get older, you can extend the amount of time you wait outside the door. A toddler can tolerate more frustration than a younger child.

- Talk to your child (and yes, your baby) about sleep. Talk to him about how peaceful the nighttime and the dark is and how rest is important to have energy to play.

- Establish a consistent bedtime and create a bedtime ritual. Include a story, quiet music, and a special stuffed animal or blanket that represents you and their closeness to you.

- You cannot be away from your children all day and expect them to separate easily from you at night when you come home: The less contact you have with your child during the day, the more contact he needs with you at night. That becomes his time to be with you.

- Be patient. It may take an hour (or more) for your child to go to sleep in the beginning. It's like a long car ride, except instead of your child saying, "Are we there yet?" it's you doing the asking.

- Even if you do everything right, getting your child to sleep and to stay asleep may still be challenging. Remember that sleep is the ultimate separation from you and real aloneness. When your child is very attached in a positive way, why should she want to be without you? The rewards of waiting and suffering a little as a sleepless parent are rich and lasting.

- Don't put your child to bed when *you're* hungry. If you come home late and you're hangry or cranky because you haven't eaten, have a quick snack so you have the energy and patience you need.

- Be aware of your anxiety. If you're anxious about separation and sleep, your child will be too.

- If your toddler climbs out of her bed and comes to you in the night, you and your partner have to decide if that works for your family. There's nothing wrong with sharing your bed, but if your child sleeping in her own bed is the goal, then you need to start the process early. Go back to her bed with her and sleep with her, as opposed to her forming a habit of coming into your bed. Whatever you decide to do, it will become what your child expects, and a difficult habit to break if you want to do so.

- When your baby or toddler has a nightmare, go to her right away. Her dreams feel very real to her; reassure her that she is safe and that dreams are not real, even though they may feel that way. Address your child's fears; children project all of their anger and aggression onto the dark. Find out what they may be angry about or afraid of, and talk with them about it.

ACKNOWLEDGMENTS

I want to thank:

Sydny Miner for collaborating with me. Her incredible writing talent, sensitivity, patience, perseverance, and belief in this book made it possible.

My agent Jane von Mehren, for her warmth, her nurturing, and expert guidance. She worked diligently to find *Being There* a great home in TarcherPerigee.

Marian Lizzi, my editor at TarcherPerigee, for believing in this book and helping bring it to fruition. I feel so grateful to have such a great team and support system.

Faith Donaldson, my research assistant, who accompanied me on this journey for the last two years, while she attended Barnard University. Her transcriptions of interviews and research help were invaluable.

My sister, psychoanalyst, writer, and teacher Karen Proner, who has always been my role model. Her depth of knowledge and expertise in the field of infant observation has always been an inspiration to me. And to my sisters Sher and Holly, who always believed in me and encouraged me in the writing of this book.

Tom Insel, former head of the National Institute of Mental Health (NIMH), for all of his support and guidance in connecting me with some of the greatest neuroscience researchers in this area of study.

Allan Schore, PhD, whose contributions to the field of relational neurobiology as well as his guidance and mentorship helped shape this book.

My colleague and fellow psychoanalyst Hope Igleheart, whose love, support, and networking on my behalf with the research attachment community was invaluable.

Gail Sheehy, whose encouragement and long discussions over many dinners helped shape my thinking about feminism.

Ellen Jacobs, for her contributions to the sections on play and for her loyal and loving friendship and collegial working relationship for the last twenty-seven years.

Graziella Pruiti, for her many years of friendship and for being my guardian angel with all legal matters pertaining to the book.

Jennifer DuBrul, whose friendship and support throughout the process of writing this book was invaluable.

Mary Cantwell, Natalie Williams, and all of the wonderful teachers and staff at the Garden House Preschool in Manhattan, for providing me such a wonderful working environment and the opportunity to help so many parents and children.

Lisa Kava and Judy Kaufman, my colleagues at Nannies Who Know, whose expertise in the field of surrogate care has given me great insight into the care of children.

Rachel Blumenthal for generously including me in the Cricket Circle community.

Jen Warner for creating a beautiful website for me and for helping me develop my social media platform.

All of the researchers who generously shared their thoughts with me: Dan Hill, Judi Mesman, Miriam and Howard Steele, Regina Sullivan, James Rilling, Tracy Bale, Charles Nelson, Steve Cole, Thomas McInerny, Randi Coen-Gilbert, Nancy Fischer Mortifee, Mary Nichols, Nim Tottenham, Joe Loizzo, Jay Belsky, Mary Gordon, Andrew Garner, and Larry Young.

All of the mothers, fathers, and young women and men who spoke to me about their feelings and experiences.

I would like to acknowledge the incredible contributions to the field of attachment and relational neurobiology of John Bowlby, Margaret Mahler, Beatrice Beebe, Ed Tronick, Mary Ainsworth, Mary Main, Dan Siegel, and Dan Stern.

I would like to thank my friends at the Aspen Institute—Walter Isaacson, Peter Reiling, Tom Loper, Bill Mayer, and Christy Orris—for providing me with an incredible opportunity to present to their community on this very important topic. And a special thank-you to my dear friend Eric Motley at the Aspen Institute, whose friendship and encouragement have been a beacon of light for me in the writing process.

And most important I would like to thank God for giving me the strength, patience, and wisdom to help my patients in pain. And to my rabbi, Ammiel Hirsch, for reminding me of the importance of spirituality and Judaism in my life, which remains a constant source of hope when helping my patients.

NOTES

Introduction

1   Division of Human Development and Disability, "Attention-Deficit/Hyperactivity Disorder (ADHD)," National Center on Birth Defects and Developmental Disabilities, Centers for Disease Control and Prevention, updated May 4, 2016, cdc.gov/ncbddd/adhd/data.html.

2   Laura A. Pratt, Debra J. Brody, and Qiuping Gu, "Antidepressant Use in Persons Aged 12 and Over: United States, 2005–2008," National Center for Health Statistics Data Brief No. 76, October 2011, Centers for Disease Control and Prevention, cdc.gov/nchs/data/databriefs/db76.htm.

3   National Association of Anorexia Nervosa and Associated Disorders, "Eating Disorder Statistics," anad.org/get-information/about-eating -disorders/eating-disorders-statistics/.

4   Eating Disorder Hope, "Statistics on Eating Disorders: Anorexia, Bulimia, Binge Eating," eatingdisorderhope.com/information/statistics-studies. Yafu Zhao and William Encinosa, "Hospitalizations for Eating Disorders from 1999 to 2006," Statistical Brief 70, April 2009, Agency for Healthcare Research and Quality, hcup-us.ahrq.gov/reports/statbriefs/sb70.jsp

5   National Center for Injury Prevention and Control, Division of Violence Prevention "Youth Violence," Centers for Disease Control and Prevention, 2012, cdc.gov/violenceprevention/pdf/yv-datasheet-a.pdf.

6   Jodi Kantor and Jessica Silver-Greenberg, "Wall Street Mothers, Stay-Home Fathers," *New York Times*, December 7, 2013, nytimes .com/2013/12/08/us/wall-street-mothers-stay-home-fathers.html.

Chapter 1 • More Is More

1   Jim Dryden, "Nurturing during Preschool Years Boosts Child's Brain
    Growth," Washington University School of Medicine, St. Louis, April 25,
    2016, medicine.wustl.edu/news/nurturing-preschool-years-boosts-childs
    -brain-growth.

2   Stanford University Medical Center, "Mom's Voice Activates Many
    Different Regions in Children's Brains, Study Shows," *Science Daily*,
    May 16, 2016, sciencedaily.com/releases/2016/05/160516181017.htm.

3   Paul Sullivan, "Investing in an Emotional Trust Fund for Your Children,"
    New York Times, June 24, 2016, nytimes.com/2016/06/25/your-money/
    investing-in-an-emotional-trust-fund-for-your-children.html.

Chapter 2 • Debunking the Myths of Modern Motherhood

1   Donald Woods Winnicott, "The Theory of the Parent-Infant Relationship,"
    International Journal of Psycho-Analysis 41 (December 1960): 585–95.

2   Jennifer Kunst, "In Search of the 'Good Enough' Mother" [blog post],
    Psychology Today, May 9, 2012, psychologytoday.com/blog/headshrinkers
    -guide-the-galaxy/201205/in-search-the-good-enough-mother.

3   Anna Freud and Dorothy Burlingham, *Infants without Families; the Case
    for and against Residential Nurseries*, 2nd ed. (New York: Medical War
    Books, International University Press, 1947).

4   Jay Belsky and David Eggebeen, "Early and Extensive Maternal
    Employment and Young Children's Socioemotional Development:
    Children of the National Longitudinal Survey of Youth," *Journal of
    Marriage and Family* 53, no. 4 (1991): 1083–98.

5   Pulsus Group, "Maternal Depression and Child Development," *Pediatrics
    & Child Health* 9, no. 8 (2004): 575–83.

6   Beatrice Beebe, Joseph Jaffe, Sara Markese, et al., "The Origins of 12-Month
     Attachment: A Microanalysis of 4-Month Mother–Infant Interaction,"
     Attachment & Human Development 12, nos. 1–2 (2010): 3–141.

7   Daniel N. Stern, *The First Relationship: Infant and Mother* (Cambridge, UK:
     Harvard University Press, 2004).

8   Konrad Lorenz, *The Year of the Greylag Goose* (London: Erye Methuen,
     1979).

9   Melanie Klein, "Mourning and Its Relation to Manic-Depressive States,"
     International Journal of Psycho-Analysis 21 (1940): 125.

10   John Bowlby, *Separation: Anxiety and Anger*, vol. 2 (New York: Basic
     Books, 1976).

11   James Robertson and Joyce Robertson, "Young Children in Brief
     Separation: A Fresh Look," *Psychoanalytic Study of the Child* 26 (1971):
     264–315.

12   Bernard Guyer, Mary Anne Freedman, Donna M. Strobino, and Edward J.
     Sondik, "Annual Summary of Vital Statistics: Trends in the Health of
     Americans During the 20th Century," *Pediatrics* 106, no. 6 (2000):
     1307–17.

13   P. Levitt, "Structural and Functional Maturation of the Developing
     Primate Brain," *Journal of Pediatrics* 143, no. 4 (October 2003): S35–S45.

14   Allan N. Schore, "The Experience-Dependent Maturation of a Regulatory
     System in the Orbital Prefrontal Cortex and the Origin of Developmental
     Psychopathology," *Development and Psychopathology* 8, no. 1 (December
     1996): 59–87.

15   John P. Trougakos, Ivona Hideg, Bonnie Hayden Cheng, and Daniel J.
     Beal, "Lunch Breaks Unpacked: The Role of Autonomy as a Moderator of
     Recovery During Lunch," *Academy of Management Journal* 57, no. 2
     (April 2014): 405–21.

16   Frank Bruni, "The Myth of Quality Time," *New York Times*, September 5,
     2015, nytimes.com/2015/09/06/opinion/sunday/frank-bruni-the-myth-of
     -quality-time.html.

17   Ibid.

18   D'Vera Cohn, Gretchen Livingston, and Wendy Wang, "How Do Mothers
     Spend Their Time at Home?," in *After Decades of Decline, A Rise in
     Stay-at-Home Mothers*, Pew Research Center Social & Demographic
     Trends, April 8, 2014, pewsocialtrends.org/2014/04/08/chapter-3-how-do
     -mothers-spend-their-time-at-home.

19   World Health Organization, "Breastfeeding," who.int/topics/breastfeeding/
     en.

20   Susan B. Neuman, Tanya Kaefer, Ashley Pinkham, and Gabrielle Strouse,
     "Can Babies Learn to Read? A Randomized Trial of Baby Media," *Journal
     of Educational Psychology* 106, no. 3 (2014): 815–30.

21   Esther Bick, "The Experience of the Skin in Early Object-Relations,"
     International Journal of Psychoanalysis 49, no. 2–3 (1968): 484–86.

22   Holly Dunsworth and Leah Eccleston, "The Evolution of Difficult
     Childbirth and Helpless Hominin Infants," *Annual Review of Anthropology*
     44 (2015): 55–69. Heinz F. R. Prechtl, "New Perspectives in Early Human
     Development," *European Journal of Obstetrics & Gynecology and
     Reproductive Biology* 21, nos. 5–6 (1986): 347–55.

23   Ruth Feldman, Magi Singer, and Orna Zagoory, "Touch Attenuates
     Infants' Physiological Reactivity to Stress," *Developmental Science* 13, no. 2
     (March 1, 2010): 271–78.

24   Stephen Suomi, "Touch and the Immune System in Rhesus Monkeys," in
     Touch in Early Development, ed. Tiffany Field (Hillsdale, NJ: Lawrence
     Eribaum Assoc., 1995): 67–79. Stephen Suomi, "Mother–Infant
     Attachment, Peer Relationships, and the Development of Social Networks
     in Rhesus Monkeys," *Human Development* 48, no. 1–2 (2005): 67–79.

25 D. Francis, J. Diorio, D. Liu, and M. J. Meaney, "Nongenomic Transmission across Generations of Maternal Behavior and Stress Responses in the Rat," *Science* 286, no. 5442 (November 1999): 1155–58.

26 "Dr. Allan Schore on Early Relationships & Lifelong Health" [interview], Let's Grow Kids, letsgrowkids.org/blog/dr-allan-schore-early-relationships -lifelong-health.

27 Grazyna Kochanska, Lea J. Boldt, Sanghag Kim, et al. "Developmental Interplay between Children's Biobehavioral Risk and the Parenting Environment from Toddler to Early School Age: Prediction of Socialization Outcomes in Preadolescence," *Development and Psychopathology* 27, no. 3 (August 2015): 775–90.

Chapter 3 • What Does It Mean to Be a Present Mother?

1 Earl K. Miller and T. J. Buschman, "Neural Mechanisms for the Executive Control of Attention," in *The Oxford Handbook of Attention*, ed. K. Nobre and S. Kastner (Oxford: Oxford University Press, 2014). Earl K. Miller and T. J. Buschman, "Cortical Circuits for the Control of Attention," *Current Opinion in Neurobiology* 23 (2013): 216–22. Robert Desimone, Earl K. Miller, and Leonardo Chelazzi, "The Interaction of Neural Systems for Attention and Memory," in *Large-Scale Theories of the Brain*, ed. Christof Koch and Joel L. Davis (Cambridge: MIT Press, 1994).

2 Beatrice Beebe and Miriam Steele. "How Does Microanalysis of Mother-Infant Communication Inform Maternal Sensitivity and Infant Attachment?" *Attachment & Human Development* 15, no. 5–6 (November 2013): 583–602.

3 Howard Steele, "Day Care and Attachment Re-Visited," *Attachment & Human Development* 10, no. 3 (September 2008): 223–23.

4 Myron A. Hofer, "Psychobiological Roots of Early Attachment," *Current Directions in Psychological Science* 15, no. 2 (April 2006): 84–88.

5   Thomas R. Insel, "A Neurobiological Basis of Social Attachment,"
     American Journal of Psychiatry 154, no. 6 (June 1997): 726–35.

6   Thomas R. Insel, Larry Young, and Zuoxin Wang, "Central Oxytocin and
     Reproductive Behaviours," *Reviews of Reproduction* 2, no. 1 (January 1997):
     28–37.

7   Insel, "A Neurobiological Basis of Social Attachment."

8   James K. Rilling and Larry J. Young, "The Biology of Mammalian
     Parenting and Its Effect on Offspring Social Development," *Science* 345,
     no. 6198 (August 2014): 771–76.

9   Thomas R. Insel and Lawrence E. Shapiro, "Oxytocin Receptor
     Distribution Reflects Social Organization in Monogamous and
     Polygamous Voles," *Proceedings of the National Academy of Sciences of the
     United States of America* 89, no. 13 (July 1992): 5981–85.

10   James K. Rilling, "The Neural and Hormonal Bases of Human Parental
     Care," *Neuropsychologia* 51, no. 4 (March 2013): 731–47.

11   James K. Rilling, Ashley C. Demarco, Patrick D. Hackett, et al., "Sex
     Differences in the Neural and Behavioral Response to Intranasal
     Oxytocin and Vasopressin During Human Social Interaction,"
     Psychoneuroendocrinology 39 (January 2014): 237–48.

12   Omri Weisman, Orna Zagoory-Sharon, and Ruth Feldman, "Oxytocin
     Administration, Salivary Testosterone, and Father–Infant Social
     Behavior," *Progress in Neuro-Psychopharmacology and Biological Psychiatry*
     49 (March 2014): 47–52.

13   Tracy L. Bale, "Sex Differences in Prenatal Epigenetic Programing of
     Stress Pathways," *Stress* 14, no. 4 (July 2011): 348–56.

14   Jim Dryden, "Nurturing during Preschool Years Boosts Child's Brain
     Growth" [news release], Washington University School of Medicine in
     St. Louis, April 25, 2016, medicine.wustl.edu/news/nurturing-preschool
     -years-boosts-childs-brain-growth.

15   Nim Tottenham, "The Importance of Early Experiences for Neuro-Affective
     Development," *Current Topics in Behavioral Neurosciences* 16 (2014): 109–29.

16   Allan N. Schore, "Effects of a Secure Attachment Relationship on Right
     Brain Development, Affect Regulation, and Infant Mental Health," *Infant
     Mental Health Journal* 22, nos. 1–2 (2001): 7–66.

17   James F. Leckman and John S. March, "Developmental Neuroscience
     Comes of Age" [editorial], *Journal of Child Psychology and Psychiatry* 52,
     no. 4 (April 2011): 333–38.

18   Andrew S. Garner, Jack P. Shonkoff, and the Committee on Psychosocial
     Aspects of Child and Family Health, Committee on Early Childhood,
     Adoption, and Dependent Care, Section on Developmental and
     Behavioral Pediatrics. "The Lifelong Effects of Early Childhood Adversity
     and Toxic Stress." *Pediatrics* 129, no. 1 (2012): e232–46.

19   Ibid.

20   Nim Tottenham and Margaret A. Sheridan, "A Review of Adversity, the
     Amygdala and the Hippocampus: A Consideration of Developmental
     Timing," *Frontiers in Human Neuroscience* 3, no. 68 (January 2010),
     doi:10.3389/neuro.09.068.2009.

21   Thomas R. Insel, James T. Winslow, Zuoxin Wang, and Larry J. Young,
     "Oxytocin, Vasopressin, and the Neuroendocrine Basis of Pair Bond
     Formation," in *Vasopressin and Oxytocin*, ed. Hans H. Zingg, Charles W.
     Bourque, and Daniel G. Bichet, *Advances in Experimental Medicine and
     Biology* 449 (New York: Springer, 1998), link.springer.com/
     chapter/10.1007/978-1-4615-4871-3_28.

22   Michael Numan and Thomas R. Insel, *The Neurobiology of Parental
     Behavior* (New York: Springer, 2003).

23   Leckman and March, "Developmental Neuroscience Comes of Age."

24   Edith Chen, Gregory E. Miller, Michael S. Kobor, and Steve W. Cole,
     "Maternal Warmth Buffers the Effects of Low Early-Life Socioeconomic

Status on Pro-Inflammatory Signaling in Adulthood," *Molecular Psychiatry* 16, no. 7 (July 2011): 729–37.

25   Grazyna Kochanska, Robert A. Philibert, and Robin A. Barry, "Interplay of Genes and Early Mother–Child Relationship in the Development of Self-Regulation from Toddler to Preschool Age," *Journal of Child Psychology and Psychiatry, and Allied Disciplines* 50, no. 11 (November 2009): 1331–38.

26   Bruno Bettelheim, *The Empty Fortress: Infantile Autism and the Birth of the Self* (New York: Free Press, 1972).

27   Jennifer M. Cernoch and Richard H. Porter, "Recognition of Maternal Axillary Odors by Infants," *Child Development* 56, no. 6 (1985): 1593–98.

28   Karen Rosenberg and Wenda Trevathan, "Bipedalism and Human Birth: The Obstetrical Dilemma Revisited," *Evolutionary Anthropology: Issues, News, and Reviews* 4, no. 5 (1995): 161–68.

29   Silva M. Bell and Mary D. Salter Ainsworth, "Infant Crying and Maternal Responsiveness," *Child Development* 43, no. 4 (December 1972): 1171–90.

30   Donald Woods Winnicott, "The Theory of the Parent-Infant Relationship," *International Journal of Psycho-Analysis* 41 (December 1960): 585–95.

31   The Commission on Children at Risk, *Hardwired to Connect: The New Scientific Case for Authoritative Communities* (New York: Broadway, 2003).

32   Suniya S. Luthar and Shawn J. Latendresse, "Children of the Affluent." *Current Directions in Psychological Science* 14, no. 1 (February 2005): 49–53.

33   Allan N. Schore, "Attachment and the Regulation of the Right Brain," *Attachment & Human Development* 2 (April 2000): 23–47, allanschore. com/pdf/SchoreAttachHumDev.pdf. Schore, "Effects of a Secure Attachment Relationship on Right Brain Development." Schore, "The Right Brain Is Dominant in Psychotherapy," *Psychotherapy* 51, no. 3 (September 2014): 388–97.

34   John Bowlby, *Attachment and Loss, Vol. I: Attachment* (New York: Basic
     Books, 1969). Bowlby, *Attachment and Loss, Vol. II: Separation* (New York:
     Basic Books, 1973).

35   Bowlby, *Attachment and Loss*, vols. I and II.

36   Peter Fonagy, György Gergely, Elliot Jurist, and Mary Target, *Affect
     Regulation, Mentalization, and the Development of Self* (New York: Other
     Press, 2005). Allan N. Schore, *Affect Regulation and the Origin of the Self:
     The Neurobiology of Emotional Development* (Hillsdale, NJ: Lawrence
     Erlbaum, 1994).

37   Bowlby, *Attachment and Loss*, vol. I. Inge Bretherton and Kristine A.
     Munholland, "Internal Working Models in Attachment Relationships:
     Elaborating a Central Construct in Attachment Theory," in *Handbook of
     Attachment: Theory, Research, and Clinical Applications*, 2nd ed., ed. J.
     Cassidy and P. R. Shaver (New York: Guilford, 2008).

38   Margaret S. Mahler, "Rapprochement Subphase of the Separation-
     Individuation Process," *Psychoanalytic Quarterly* 41, no. 4 (October 1972):
     487–506.

39   Jay Belsky and Michael J. Rovine, "Nonmaternal Care in the First Year of
     Life and the Security of Infant-Parent Attachment," *Child Development* 59,
     no. 1 (1988): 157–67.

40   Mary D. Salter Ainsworth, Mary C. Blehar, Everett Waters, and Sally N.
     Wall, *Patterns of Attachment: A Psychological Study of the Strange Situation*
     (New York: Psychology Press, 2015).

41   Beatrice Beebe and Frank M. Lachmann, *The Origins of Attachment:
     Infant Research and Adult Treatment* (London: Routledge, 2014).

42   Salter Ainsworth, et al., *Patterns of Attachment*.

43   Peter Fonagy and Mary Target, "Attachment and Reflective Function:
     Their Role in Self-Organization," *Development and Psychopathology* 9
     (1997): 679–700.

44   Kathy Brous, "The Adult Attachment Interview (AAI): Mary Main in a
     Strange Situation," *Attachment Disorder Healing*, March 21, 2014,
     attachmentdisorderhealing.com/adult-attachment-interview-aai-mary
     -main.

45   Mary E. Connors, "The Renunciation of Love: Dismissive Attachment
     and Its Treatment," *Psychoanalytic Psychology* 14, no. 4 (1997): 475–93.

46   Allan N. Schore, "Advances in Neuropsychoanalysis, Attachment Theory,
     and Trauma Research: Implications for Self Psychology," *Psychoanalytic
     Inquiry* 22 (2002): 433–84.

47   Donald Woods Winnicott, *The Maturational Processes and the Facilitating
     Environment: Studies in the Theory of Emotional Development* (London:
     The Hogarth Press and the Institute of Psychoanalysis, 1965).

48   Bowlby, *Attachment and Loss*, vol. I. John Bowlby, *A Secure Base: Parent-
     Child Attachment and Healthy Human Development* (London: Routledge,
     1988).

Chapter 4 • Presence 101

1   Joe Loizzo, Robert A. F. Thurman, and Daniel J. Siegel, *Sustainable
     Happiness: The Mind Science of Well-Being, Altruism, and Inspiration* (New
     York: Routledge, 2012).

2   Ram Dass, *Journey of Awakening: A Meditator's Guidebook*, ed. Daniel
     Goleman, Dwarkanath Bonner, and Dale Borglum (New York: Bantam,
     1990).

3   Chen Yu and Linda B. Smith, "The Social Origins of Sustained Attention
     in One-Year-Old Human Infants," *Current Biology* 26, no. 9 (2016): 1235–40.

4   James J. Newham, Anja Wittkowski, Janine Hurley, et al., "Effects of
     Antenatal Yoga on Maternal Anxiety and Depression: A Randomized
     Controlled Trial," *Depression and Anxiety* 31, no. 8 (April 2014): 631–40.

5   Victoria J. Bourne and Brenda K. Todd, "When Left Means Right: An
     Explanation of the Left Cradling Bias in Terms of Right Hemisphere
     Specializations," *Developmental Science* 7, no. 1 (February 2004): 19–24.

6   Nim Tottenham, "Human Amygdala Development in the Absence of
     Species-Expected Caregiving," *Developmental Psychobiology* 54, no. 6
     (September 2012): 598–611. Nim Tottenham. "The Importance of Early
     Experiences for Neuro-Affective Development." *Current Topics in
     Behavioral Neurosciences* 16 (2014): 109–29.

7   Judi Mesman, Marinus van IJzendoorn, Kazuko Behrens, et al., "Is the
     Ideal Mother a Sensitive Mother? Beliefs about Early Childhood Parenting
     in Mothers across the Globe," *International Journal of Behavioral
     Development* 40, no. 5 (September 2016): 385–97.

8   Sunaina Seth, Andrew J. Lewis, and Megan Galbally, "Perinatal Maternal
     Depression and Cortisol Function in Pregnancy and the Postpartum
     Period: A Systematic Literature Review," *BMC Pregnancy Childbirth* 16,
     no. 1 (2016): 124–43.

9   Brenda L. Volling, Nancy L. McElwain, Paul C. Notaro, and Carla
     Herrera, "Parents' Emotional Availability and Infant Emotional
     Competence: Predictors of Parent–Infant Attachment and Emerging Self-
     Regulation," *Journal of Family Psychology* 16, no. 4 (2002): 447–65.

10   Daniel Hill, *Affect Regulation Theory: A Clinical Model* (New York:
     W. W. Norton, 2015).

11   Margaret S. Mahler, Fred Pine, and Anni Bergman, *The Psychological Birth
     of the Human Infant Symbiosis and Individuation* (New York: Basic Books,
     2000).

12   Ibid.

13   Mary D. Ainsworth, *Infancy in Uganda: Infant Care and the Growth of Love*
     (Baltimore, MD: Johns Hopkins University Press, 1967).

14 Judi Mesman, et al., "Is the Ideal Mother a Sensitive Mother?" Rosanneke,
    A. G. Emmen, Maike Malda, et al., "Sensitive Parenting as a Cross-
    Cultural Ideal: Sensitivity Beliefs of Dutch, Moroccan, and Turkish
    Mothers in the Netherlands," *Attachment & Human Development* 14, no. 6
    (2012): 601–19.

15 Elizabeth Higley and Mary Dozier, "Nighttime Maternal Responsiveness
    and Infant Attachment at One Year," *Attachment & Human Development*
    11, no. 4 (July 2009): 347–63.

16 David Waynforth, "The Influence of Parent-Infant Cosleeping, Nursing,
    and Childcare on Cortisol and SIgA Immunity in a Sample of British
    Children," *Developmental Psychobiology* 49, no. 6 (2007): 640–48.

17 Roseriet Beijers, J. Marianne Riksen-Walraven, and Carolina de Weerth,
    "Cortisol Regulation in 12-Month-Old Human Infants: Associations with
    the Infants' Early History of Breastfeeding and Co-Sleeping," *Stress* 16,
    no. 3 (2013): 267–77. Alan R. Wiesenfeld, Carol Zander Malatesta, Patricia
    B. Whitman, et al., "Psychophysiological Response of Breast- and Bottle-
    Feeding Mothers to Their Infants' Signals," *Psychophysiology* 22, no. 1
    (1985): 79–86.

Chapter 5 • Making It Better

1   Edward Tronick, *The Neurobehavioral and Social-Emotional Development of
    Infants and Children* (New York: Norton, 2007).

2   Jeffrey F. Cohn and Edward Z. Tronick, "Three-Month-Old Infants'
    Reaction to Simulated Maternal Depression," *Child Development* 54, no. 1
    (February 1983): 185–93. Edward Tronick, Heidelise Als, Lauren Adamson,
    et al., "The Infant's Response to Entrapment between Contradictory
    Messages in Face-to-Face Interaction," *Journal of the American Academy of
    Child Psychiatry* 17, no. 1 (1978): 1–13.

3   Mary D. Salter Ainsworth and Silvia M. Bell, "Attachment, Exploration,
    and Separation: Illustrated by the Behavior of One-Year-Olds in a Strange

Situation," *Child Development* 41, no. 1 (1970): 49–67. Mary D. Salter Ainsworth, Mary C. Blehar, Everett Waters, and Sally N. Wall, *Patterns of Attachment: A Psychological Study of the Strange Situation.* (New York: Psychology Press, 2015).

4   Suniya S. Luthar and Shawn J. Latendresse, "Children of the Affluent," *Current Directions in Psychological Science* 14, no. 1 (February 2005): 49–53.

5   Elizabeth Higley and Mary Dozier, "Nighttime Maternal Responsiveness and Infant Attachment at One Year," *Attachment & Human Development* 11, no. 4 (July 2009): 347–63.

6   Ora Aviezer, Abraham Sagi, Tirtsa Joels, and Yair Ziv, "Emotional Availability and Attachment Representations in Kibbutz Infants and Their Mothers," *Developmental Psychology* 35, no. 3 (1999): 811–21.

Chapter 6   •   When You Can't Be There

1   Susan W. Coates, "John Bowlby and Margaret S. Mahler: Their Lives and Theories," *Journal of the American Psychoanalytic Association* 52, no. 2 (2004): 571–601.

2   Alyssa Pozniak, Katherine Wen, Krista Olson, et al., "Family and Medical Leave in 2012: Detailed Results Appendix," Abt Associates, September 6, 2012, rev. April 18, 2014, dol.gov/asp/evaluation/fmla/FMLA-Detailed -Results-Appendix.pdf. Emily Peck, "One-Quarter of Mothers Return to Work Less Than 2 Weeks After Giving Birth, Report Finds," *Huffington Post*, updated August 19, 2015, huffingtonpost.com/entry/nearly-1-in-4 -new-mothers-return-to-work-less-than-2-weeks-after-giving-birth_ us_55d308aae4b0ab468d9e3e37.

3   Jennifer S. Mascaro, Patrick D. Hackett, and James K. Rilling, "Testicular Volume Is Inversely Correlated with Nurturing-Related Brain Activity in Human Fathers," *Proceedings of the National Academy of Sciences of the United States of America* 110, no. 39 (September 2013): 15746–51.

4   Ruth Feldman, Ilanit Gordon, Inna Schneiderman, et al., "Natural
     Variations in Maternal and Paternal Care Are Associated with Systematic
     Changes in Oxytocin following Parent–Infant Contact,"
     Psychoneuroendocrinology 35, no. 8 (September 2010): 1133–41.

5   "Buzzing Flies More Likely to Wake Men Than Crying Babies: Study," *The
     Telegraph*, November 29, 2009, telegraph.co.uk/news/newstopics/howabout
     that/6684362/Buzzing-flies-more-likely-to-wake-men-than-crying-babies
     -study.html.

6   Ibid.

7   Jonathan Cohn, "The Hell of American Daycare," *New Republic*, April 15,
     2015, newrepublic.com/article/112892/hell-american-day-care.

8   Community Child Care Council of Santa Clara County, "Regulation and
     Licensing of Child Care Programs in California," d3n8a8pro7vhmx
     .cloudfront.net/rrnetwork/pages/78/attachments/original/1451607399/CA
     _Licensing_Regulations_Compare.pdf?1451607399.

9   Ohio Department of Jobs and Family Services, "Required Staff/Child
     Ratios for Child Care Centers," March 2006, odjfs.state.oh.us/forms/file
     .asp?id=245&type=application/pdf.

10   Alan Stein, Lars-Erik Malmberg, Penelope Leach, et al., "The Influence of
     Different Forms of Early Childcare on Children's Emotional and
     Behavioural Development at School Entry," *Child: Care, Health and
     Development* 39, no. 5 (September 2013): 676–87.

11   National Resource Center for Health and Safety in Child Care and Early
     Education, "Staffing: Ratios for Small Family Child Care Homes," August
     18, 2016, cfoc.nrckids.org/StandardView/1.1.1.

Chapter 7 • Understanding the Costs of Being Absent

1   Marinus H. van IJzendoorn, Carlo Schuengel, and Marian J. Bakermans-Kranenburg, "Disorganized Attachment in Early Childhood: Meta-Analysis of Precursors, Concomitants, and Sequelae," *Development and Psychopathology* 11, no. 2 (1999): 225–50. Geert-Jan J. M. Stams, Femmie Juffer, and Marinus H. van IJzendoorn, "Maternal Sensitivity, Infant Attachment, and Temperament in Early Childhood Predict Adjustment in Middle Childhood: The Case of Adopted Children and Their Biologically Unrelated Parents," *Developmental Psychology* 38, no. 5 (2002): 806.

2   "Understanding the Stress Response," Harvard Health Publications, updated March 18, 2016, health.harvard.edu/staying-healthy/understanding-the-stress-response. Michael Randall, "The Physiology of Stress: Cortisol and the Hypothalamic-Pituitary-Adrenal Axis," *Dartmouth Undergraduate Journal of Science*, February 3, 2011, dujs.dartmouth.edu/2011/02/the-physiology-of-stress-cortisol-and-the-hypothalamic-pituitary-adrenal-axis.

3   Megan R. Gunnar, Erin Kryzer, Mark J. Van Ryzin, and Deborah A. Phillips, "The Rise in Cortisol in Family Daycare: Associations with Aspects of Care Quality, Child Behavior, and Child Sex," *Child Development* 81, no. 3 (2010): 851–69.

4   Emma C. Sarro, Donald A. Wilson, and Regina M. Sullivan, "Maternal Regulation of Infant Brain State," *Current Biology* 24, no. 14 (July 2014): 1664–69. Regina M. Sullivan, "The Neurobiology of Attachment to Nurturing and Abusive Caregivers," *Hastings Law Journal* 63, no. 6 (August 2012): 1553–70. G. Barr, S. Moriceau, K. Shionoya, et al., "Transitions in Infant Attachment during a Sensitive Period Is Modulated by Dopamine in the Amygdala," *Nature Neuroscience* 12 (2009): 1367–69. S. Moriceau and Regina M. Sullivan, "Maternal Presence Serves to Switch between Attraction and Fear in Infancy," *Nature Neuroscience* 9 (2006):

1004–06. K. Shionoya, S. Moriceau, P. Bradstock, and Regina M. Sullivan. "Maternal Attenuation of Hypothalamic Paraventricular Nucleus Norepinephrine Switches Avoidance Learning to Preference Learning in Preweanling Rat Pups," *Hormones & Behavior* 52 (2007): 391–400.

5   Michael D. De Bellis, "The Psychobiology of Neglect," *Child Maltreatment* 10, no. 2 (2005): 150–72.

6   Child Mind Institute, "2016 Children's Mental Health Report," childmind .org/report/2016-childrens-mental-health-report.

7   Shaozheng Qin, Christina B. Young, Xujun Duan, et al., "Amygdala Subregional Structure and Intrinsic Functional Connectivity Predicts Individual Differences in Anxiety during Early Childhood," *Biological Psychiatry* 75, no. 11 (2014): 892–900.

8   Mark W. Gilbertson, Martha E. Shenton, Aleksandra Ciszewski, et al., "Smaller Hippocampal Volume Predicts Pathologic Vulnerability to Psychological Trauma," *Nature Neuroscience* 5, no. 11 (2002): 1242–47. Rajendra A. Morey, Andrea L. Gold, Kevin S. LaBar, et al., "Amygdala Volume Changes in Posttraumatic Stress Disorder in a Large Case-Controlled Veterans Group," *Archives of General Psychiatry* 69, no. 11 (2012): 1169–78. Mark A. Rogers, Hidenori Yamasue, Osamu Abe, et al., "Smaller Amygdala Volume and Reduced Anterior Cingulate Gray Matter Density Associated with History of Post-Traumatic Stress Disorder," *Psychiatry Research: Neuroimaging* 174, no. 3 (2009): 210–16.

9   Centers for Disease Control and Prevention, "Attention-Deficit/Hyperactivity Disorder (ADHD)," updated May 4, 2016, cdc.gov/ncbddd/adhd/ data.html.

10   Marilyn Wedge, "Why French Kids Don't Have ADHD," *Psychology Today*, March 8, 2012, psychologytoday.com/blog/suffer-the-children/201203/ why-french-kids-dont-have-adhd.

11   National Institute of Mental Health, "Prescribed Stimulant Use for ADHD Continues to Rise Steadily," September 28, 2011, nimh.nih.gov/

news/science-news/2011/prescribed-stimulant-use-for-adhd-continues-to
-rise-steadily.shtml.

12   Child Mind Institute, "2016 Children's Mental Health Report."

13   Deborah Lowe Vandell and Mary Anne Corasaniti, "Variations in Early
     Child Care: Do They Predict Subsequent Social, Emotional, and
     Cognitive Differences?," *Early Childhood Research Quarterly* 5, no. 4 (1990):
     555–72. John E. Bates, Denny Marvinney, Timothy Kelly, et al., "Child-
     Care History and Kindergarten Adjustment," *Developmental Psychology* 30,
     no. 5 (1994): 690–700. Neal W. Finkelstein, "Aggression: Is It Stimulated
     by Day Care?," *Young Children* 37 (August 1982): 3–9. Jay Belsky,
     "Developmental Risks Associated with Infant Day Care: Attachment
     Insecurity, Noncompliance, and Aggression?," in *Psychosocial Issues in Day
     Care*, Shahla Chebbrazi, ed. (Washington, DC: American Psychiatric
     Press, 1990): 37–68. Jay Belsky, "Early Day Care and Infant-Mother
     Attachment Security," *Encyclopedia on Early Childhood Development*,
     updated May 2012, child-encyclopedia.com/attachment/according-experts/
     early-day-care-and-infant-mother-attachment-security.

14   Maurizio Pompili, Iginia Mancinelli, Paolo Girardi, et al., "Childhood
     Suicide: A Major Issue in Pediatric Health Care," *Issues in Comprehensive
     Pediatric Nursing* 28 (1): 63–68.

15   John Bowlby, "Grief and Mourning in Infancy and Early Childhood,"
     Psychoanalytic Study of the Child 15, no. 1 (1960): 9–52.

16   Meera E. Modi and Larry J. Young, "The Oxytocin System in Drug
     Discovery for Autism: Animal Models and Novel Therapeutic Strategies,"
     Hormones and Behavior 61, no. 3 (March 2012): 340–50.

17   Masaya Tachibana, Kuriko Kagitani-Shimono, Ikuko Mohri, et al.,
     "Long-Term Administration of Intranasal Oxytocin Is a Safe and
     Promising Therapy for Early Adolescent Boys with Autism Spectrum
     Disorders," *Journal of Child and Adolescent Psychopharmacology* 23, no. 2
     (2013): 123–27.

18 Charles A. Nelson, Nathan A. Fox, and Charles H. Zeanah, *Romania's Abandoned Children: Deprivation, Brain Development, and the Struggle for Recovery* (Cambridge: Harvard University Press, 2014).

19 Darlene Francis, Josie Diorio, Dong Liu, and Michael J. Meaney, "Nongenomic Transmission across Generations of Maternal Behavior and Stress Responses in the Rat," *Science* 286, no. 5442 (1999): 1155–58.

20 John Bowlby, *Attachment and Loss, Vol. II: Separation* (New York: Basic Books, 1973). Mark H. Bickhard, "Scaffolding and Self Scaffolding: Central Aspects of Development," *Chz'ldreri'sd U* 610 (2013): 33–52.

21 Constance Hammen, Julienne E. Bower, and Steven W. Cole, "Oxytocin Receptor Gene Variation and Differential Susceptibility to Family Environment in Predicting Youth Borderline Symptoms," *Journal of Personality Disorders* 29, no. 2 (2015): 177–92.

22 Kathleen Ries Merikangas, Jian-ping He, Marcy Burstein, et al., "Lifetime Prevalence of Mental Disorders in US Adolescents: Results from the National Comorbidity Survey Replication–Adolescent Supplement (NCS-A)," *Journal of the American Academy of Child & Adolescent Psychiatry* 49, no. 10 (2010): 980–89.

23 The Renfrew Center Foundation for Eating Disorders, "Eating Disorders 101 Guide: A Summary of Issues," *Statistics and Resources*, 2003.

24 The National Center on Addiction and Substance Abuse, "National Study Reveals: Teen Substance Use America's #1 Public Health Problem," June 29, 2011, centeronaddiction.org/newsroom/press-releases/national -study-reveals-teen-substance-use-americas-1-public-health-problem.

25 Michael Numan and Thomas R. Insel, *The Neurobiology of Parental Behavior* (New York: Springer, 2003).

26 Anne Buist, "Childhood Abuse, Parenting and Postpartum Depression," *Australian and New Zealand Journal of Psychiatry* 32, no. 4 (August 1998): 479–87.

Chapter 8 • When Mothers Turn Away

1   Erik H. Erikson, *Identity and the Life Cycle* (New York: W. W. Norton, 1994).

2   Sigmund Freud, "On Psychotherapy," in *The Standard Edition of the Complete Psychological Works of Sigmund Freud, Vol. 7: A Case of Hysteria, Three Essays and Other Works* (1901–1905), eds. James Strachey, Anna Freud, Carrie Lee Rothgeb, Angela Richards, and the Scientific Literature Corporation (London: Hogarth Press, 1953–74).

3   D. Francis, J. Diorio, D. Liu, and M. J. Meaney, "Nongenomic Transmission across Generations of Maternal Behavior and Stress Responses in the Rat," *Science* 286, no. 5442 (November 1999): 1155–58. Michael Numan and Thomas R. Insel, *The Neurobiology of Parental Behavior* (New York: Springer, 2003).

4   Dan Hurley, "Grandma's Experiences Leave Epigenetic Mark on Your Genes," *Discover*, June 25, 2015, discovermagazine.com/2013/may/13 -grandmas-experiences-leave-epigenetic-mark-on-your-genes.

5   Harry F. Harlow, Margaret K. Harlow, Robert O. Dodsworth, and G. L. Arling, "Maternal Behavior of Rhesus Monkeys Deprived of Mothering and Peer Associations in Infancy," *Proceedings of the American Philosophical Society* 110, no. 1 (1966): 58–66.

6   Marian Radke-Yarrow, Carolyn Zahn-Waxler, Dorothy T. Richardson, et al., "Caring Behavior in Children of Clinically Depressed and Well Mothers," *Child Development* 65, no. 5 (October 1994): 1405–14.

7   Marian Radke-Yarrow, *Children of Depressed Mothers: From Early Childhood to Maturity* (New York: Cambridge University Press, 1998).

8   Les B. Whitbeck, Dan R. Hoyt, Ronald L. Simons, et al., "Intergenerational Continuity of Parental Rejection and Depressed Affect," *Journal of Personality and Social Psychology* 63, no. 6 (1992): 1036.

9   Charles A. Nelson, Nathan A. Fox, and Charles H. Zeanah, *Romania's Abandoned Children: Deprivation, Brain Development, and the Struggle for Recovery* (Cambridge: Harvard University Press, 2014).

10   Centers for Disease Control and Prevention, "Prevalence of Self-Reported Postpartum Depressive Symptoms—17 States, 2004–2005," *Morbidity and Mortality Weekly Report* 57, no. 14 (April 2008): 361–66.

11   Sheila Shribman and Kate Billingham, *Healthy Child Programme: Pregnancy and the First Five Years* (London: COI for the Department of Health, 2009).

Chapter 9 • Why Don't We Value Mothering?

1   Nicole Lyn Pesce, "Beyoncé Calls Blue Ivy Her Greatest Accomplishment," *NY Daily News*, March 10, 2016, nydailynews.com/entertainment/music/beyonce-calls-blue-ivy-greatest-accomplishment-article-1.2559619.

2   Jenny Kutner, "Beyoncé Said Being a Mom Is Her Greatest Accomplishment," Mic, March 11, 2016, mic.com/articles/137669/beyonc-said-being-a-mom-is-her-greatest-accomplishment-um-really-bey#.qhIEqUOlG.

3   Elizabeth Kiefer, "Beyoncé Is under Fire for Saying Motherhood Is Her Biggest Accomplishment," Refinery29, March 11, 2016, refinery29.com/2016/03/105797/beyonce-proudest-accomplishment-motherhood.

4   Judith Shulevitz, "How to Fix Feminism," *New York Times*, June 10, 2016, nytimes.com/2016/06/12/opinion/sunday/how-to-fix-feminism.html.

5   Fareed Zakaria, *Anne-Marie Slaughter Talks Women in the Workplace*, [video; interview], October 17, 2015, cnn.com/videos/tv/2015/10/17/exp-gps-slaughter-sot-women-at-work.cnn.

6   Francine D. Blau and Lawrence M. Kahn, "The Gender Wage Gap: Extent, Trends, and Explanations," Working Paper, no. 21913, National Bureau of Economic Research, January 2016, nber.org/papers/w21913.

7   Claire Cain Miller and David Streitfeld, "Big Leaps for Parental Leave, if
     Workers Actually Take It," *New York Times*, September 1, 2015, nytimes
     .com/2015/09/02/upshot/big-leaps-for-parental-leave-if-workers-actually
     -follow-through.html.

8   Pew Research Center, "Fewer Mothers Prefer Full-Time Work," Pew
     Research Center's Social & Demographic Trends, July 12, 2007,
     pewsocialtrends.org/2007/07/12/fewer-mothers-prefer-full-time-work.

9   George E. Vaillant, *Triumphs of Experience: The Men of the Harvard Grant
     Study* (Cambridge, MA: Belknap Press, 2012).

10   Pew Research Center, "Millennials: Confident. Connected. Open to
     Change," Pew Research Center's Social & Demographic Trends, February
     24, 2010, www.pewsocialtrends.org/2010/02/24/millennials-confident
     -connected-open-to-change.

11   Pew Research Center, "The Rise in Dual Income Households," June 18,
     2015, pewresearch.org/ft_dual-income-households-1960-2012-2.

12   Salary.com, "2013 What's a Mom Worth Infographics," salary.com/2013
     -mom-infographics. Aaron Gouveia, "How Much Money Should Moms Be
     Paid?," Salary.com, salary.com/how-much-should-moms-be-paid/slide/13.

13   Madeline Levine, *The Price of Privilege: How Parental Pressure and Material
     Advantage Are Creating a Generation of Disconnected and Unhappy Kids.*
     (New York: Harper Perennial, 2008).

Chapter 10   •   Where Do We Go from Here?

1   U.S. Department of Labor, "Family and Medical Leave Act—Wage and
     Hour Division (WHD)," dol.gov/whd/fmla.

2   Laura Addati, Naomi Cassirer, and Katherine Gilchrist, *Maternity and
     Paternity at Work: Law and Practice Across the World*, May 13, 2014, ilo.org/
     global/publications/ilo-bookstore/order-online/books/WCMS_242615/
     lang--en/index.htm.

3   Pedro Manuel Carneiro, Katrine Vellesen Løken, and Kjell G. Salvanes,
     "A Flying Start? Long Term Consequences of Maternal Time Investments
     in Children during Their First Year of Life," SSRN Scholarly Paper ID
     1714896, Social Science Research Network, October 2010, iza.org/dp5362
     .pdf.

4   Marshall Bright, "Etsy Announces New Parental Leave Policy,"
     Refinery29, March 15, 2016, refinery29.com/2016/03/106024/etsy-parental
     -leave-policy.

5   National Institute of Mental Health, "Any Disorder Among Children," nimh
     .nih.gov/health/statistics/prevalence/any-disorder-among-children.shtml.

6   Centers for Disease Control and Prevention, "About the CDC-Kaiser ACE
     Study," cdc.gov/violenceprevention/acestudy/about.html.

7   U.S. Department of Labor, "Family and Medical Leave Act."

8   Richard Branson, "Why Virgin Is Extending Shared Parental Leave," June
     10, 2015, virgin.com/richard-branson/why-virgin-is-extending-shared
     -parental-leave. Cranz, Tawni, "Starting Now at Netflix: Unlimited
     Maternity and Paternity Leave," Netflix Media Center, August 4, 2015,
     media.netflix.com/en/company-blog/starting-now-at-netflix-unlimited
     -maternity-and-paternity-leave.

9   Zlata Rodionova, "Google's Paid Maternity Leave Has Halved the Number
     of New Mothers Quitting," Independent, January 29, 2016, independent.
     co.uk/news/business/google-s-paid-maternity-leave-halved-the-number-of
     -new-mothers-quitting-youtube-ceo-says-a6841326.html.

10   Heather Boushey and Sarah Jane Glynn, "There Are Significant Business
     Costs to Replacing Employees," Center for American Progress, November
     16, 2012, americanprogress.org/issues/labor/report/2012/11/16/44464/there
     -are-significant-business-costs-to-replacing-employees.

11   Anne-Marie Slaughter, Unfinished Business: Women Men Work Family
     (New York: Random House, 2015).

12   Gretchen Livingston, "Growing Number of Dads Home with the Kids,"
      Pew Research Center's Social & Demographic Trends, June 5, 2014,
      pewsocialtrends.org/2014/06/05/growing-number-of-dads-home-with-the
      -kids.

13   Lydia Dishman. "What's Missing from Amazon's New Parental Leave
      Policy," Fast Company, November 3, 2015, fastcompany.com/3053093/
      second-shift/whats-missing-from-amazons-new-parental-leave-policy.

14   U.S. Congress, "H.R.3377—Social Security Caregiver Credit Act of 2015,"
      July 29, 2015, www.congress.gov/bill/114th-congress/house-bill/3377. Nita
      Lowery, "Lowey Introduces Legislation to Provide Social Security Earnings
      Credit to Caregivers" [press release], August 27, 2015, lowey.house.gov/
      media-center/press-releases/lowey-introduces-legislation-provide-social
      -security-earnings-credit.

15   National Partnership for Women & Families, "Family and Medical
      Insurance Leave (FAMILY) Act," nationalpartnership.org/issues/work
      -family/family-act.html. K. J. Dell'Antonia, "New Act Proposes National
      Paid Family Leave Policy" [blog post], New York Times, December 11, 2013,
      parenting.blogs.nytimes.com/2013/12/11/new-act-proposes-national-paid
      -family-leave-policy.

INDEX

absence of mothers, costs of, 143–63
  for adolescents and adults, 161–63
  aggression and behavioral problems,
    150–55
  attentional difficulties, 145–50
  lack of resilience to stress, 159–60
  social difficulties, 157–59
abuse and neglect of children, 46, 144,
  154
Adderall prescriptions, 148–49
addictions, 143, 160, 163
adolescents, 161–63, 211–13
adopted children, 46, 122
adoptive and foster parents, 46
Adult Attachment Interview (AAI), 63
adults, effects of absence on, 161–63
Adverse Childhood Experience Survey,
  203
Affect Regulation Theory (Hill), 187
affluent families, 52, 111, 196, 197–98
Agency for Healthcare Research and
  Quality, xiv
aggression
  and acknowledgment of children's
    feelings, 117–18
  and chronic anxiety, 147
  and costs of absence, 150–55
  and daycares/preschools, 60, 152–53,
    154
  defensive, 152
  and early experiences with mother,
    143
  and emotional absence, 53–54
  gender differences in, 154–55
  increase in incidence of, xiii, xiv

  and insecure avoidant attachment, 62
  internalization of, 155
  and low tolerance for frustration, 152
  as maladaptive defense, 49
  normal amounts of, 151
  and playing with children, 88
  as result of premature separation, 153
  as sign of anxiety or depression, 153
  in toddlers, 79–80, 150
Ainsworth, Mary, 35, 47, 60, 61, 63, 94,
  108–9
alleles, 44
alloparental model of parenting,
  121–22, 127
Amazon, 207
ambivalence of mothers
  addressing, 182
  and desire to return to work, 193
  ignoring signs of, 82
  increase in prevalence of, 168
  mothers' down playing of, 180
  and neurotic repetition, 168–69
  risks associated with, 164
  self-awareness of, 180
  shame associated with, 181
  as sign of postpartum depression, 20
amygdala, 40, 146, 147–48, 156
anger
  and acknowledgment of children's
    feelings, 117–18
  of crying babies, 151
  and disorganized mothers, 66
  and insecure avoidant attachment,
    62
  internalization of, 151

Coen-Gilbert, Randi, 72
cognitive behavioral therapy, 163
cognitive development, early
    encouragement of, 26–27
Cohn, Jonathan, 137
Cole, Steve, 44, 160
colic, 30, 45, 150
Commission on Children at Risk, 49
communication between mothers and
    babies, 78–79
competitiveness in children, 89
Connors, Mary, 64
co-parenting arrangements, 103
coping mechanisms, 155, 163
corporate cultures, 6
corticosterone production, 39
cortisol
    and autism spectrum, 157
    and brain development, 28
    and chronic stress, 147
    and co-sleeping, 97
    effect of physical contact on, 28
    and fight-or-flight response, 145–46,
        147
    and gender differences, 149
    and maternal absence, 146
    and yoga, 72
co-sleeping, 97–98, 112
counseling, 82
cradling babies in left arm, 74
crying
    and anger experienced by babies, 151
    causes of, 84
    and colic, 30, 45, 150
    "crying it out," 83
    and fathers as primary caregivers, 124
    and fears of children, 98
    and frustration of babies, 29, 83–84
    inattention of mother to, 156
    as means of communication, 28, 29
    and needs of children, 28
    responding to, 47, 83–84
    and secure mothers, 63
    and sleep training, 228

Dass, Ram, 69
daycares and preschools, 136–40
    and aggression, 60, 152–53, 154
    costs of, 197
    and duration of separation, 22
    and feminism, 187
    reliance of families on, 121
    sharing a caregiver as alternative to,
        138
defenses developed by children, 49, 53
defensive (or stress-inoculated)
    independence, 170
DeLauro, Rosa, 210
dependency
    and bonding imperative, 47
    as bridge to healthy separation, 57, 58
    and dismissive mothers, 64
    fear of, 64
    and later independence, 29–30
depression
    and ADD/ADHD diagnoses, 148
    of adolescents, 163
    aggression as sign of, 153
    boredom as sign of, 20–21
    and chronic stress response, 148, 156
    as consequence of absence, 14,
        155–56
    and defensive independence, 170
    and disorganized mothers, 66
    and early experiences with mother,
        143
    gender differences in, 155
    increase in incidence of, xiii
    and inflammatory signals, 44
    and internalization of aggression or
        fear, 151, 155
    and lack of resilience to stress, 160
    maternal, 20–21, 154 (see also
        postpartum depression)
    and repressed emotions, 172
    and resilience to stress, 42
    and talking to children, 84
deprivation, 169
devices, unplugging from, 69–72, 110

ABOUT THE AUTHORS

Erica Komisar, LCSW, is a psychoanalyst and parent guidance expert who has been in private practice in New York City for twenty-four years. She received her BA from Georgetown University, an MSW from Columbia University, and graduated from the New York Freudian Society as a psychoanalyst in 1999.

Ms. Komisar began her career as a clinical social worker, working with families and children from diverse socioeconomic and racial backgrounds in clinics in Brooklyn and Manhattan, where she designed and delivered parenting education seminars. In 1992 she started a training and development company to bring parenting workshops and work/family life seminars to corporations including Goldman Sachs and Sherman and Sterling. She is the psychological consultant to the Garden House Preschool in Manhattan. In addition to helping parents whose children may be struggling with emotional and behavioral issues, she also treats adults and adolescents who suffer from depression, anxiety, and a variety of eating disorders and addictions in her private practice.

Sydny Miner is a writer and publishing industry veteran who has worked on numerous bestselling and award-winning titles.